NOTTINGHAM TO LINCOLN

Vic Mitchell and Keith Smith

MP Middleton Press

Front cover: Passing through Swinderby on 3rd March 2007 is class V1 2-6-2 no. 4771 Green Arrow, in its original livery. It is hauling a tour train, bound for the Grimsby area. (H.Ballantyne)

Back cover: Pictured at Southwell on 29th May 1959 is ex-Midland Railway 0-4-4T no. 58065. It was the last of its type in use and hauled the final train on the branch in the following month. (R.C.Riley/M.J.Stretton coll.)

Back cover lower: A class 170 DMU rumbles over the Trent Dyke near Newark, bound for Lincoln on 31st March 2007. In the background is the massive factory of the British Sugar Corporation at Kelham. (J.Whitehouse)

CAB RIDE

The DVD *Leicester to Lincoln* includes a 50-minute journey over the route in 2008. It is available from Middleton Press.

Published June 2013

ISBN 978 1 908174 43 7

© *Middleton Press, 2013*

Design Deborah Esher
Typesetting Barbara Mitchell

Published by
    Middleton Press
    Easebourne Lane
    Midhurst
    West Sussex
    GU29 9AZ
Tel: 01730 813169
Fax: 01730 812601
Email: info@middletonpress.co.uk
www.middletonpress.co.uk

Printed in the United Kingdom by Henry Ling Limited, at the Dorset Press, Dorchester, DT1 1HD

INDEX

ACKNOWLEDGEMENTS

We are very grateful for the assistance received from many of those mentioned in the credits, also to A.R.Carder, A.J.Castledine, G.Croughton, M.Dart, F.Hornby, S.C.Jenkins, P.Kelly, D.K.Jones, N.Langridge, Mr D. and Dr S.Salter, M.Turvey, T.Walsh, E.Wilmshurst and in particular, our always supportive wives, Barbara Mitchell and Janet Smith.

I. Railway Clearing House map for 1947.
The connection above Fiskerton was in use in 1925-1965.

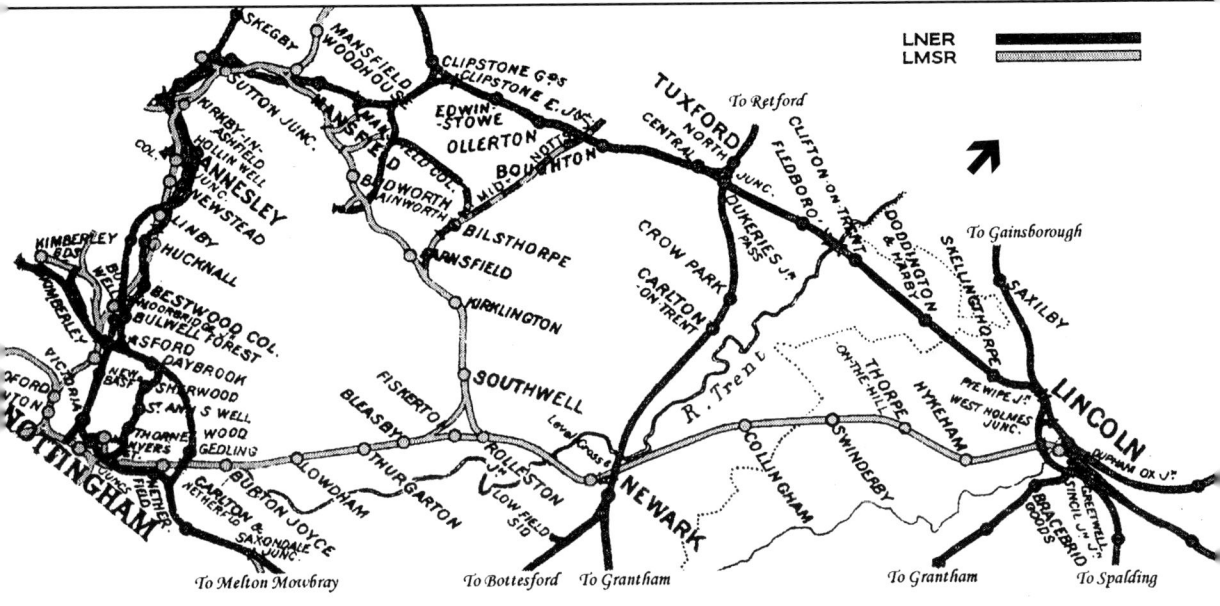

GEOGRAPHICAL SETTING

The route from Nottingham to Lincoln runs northeast, the initial part being over red sandstones. Collieries were sunk near Blidworth around 1930 and form part of the East Midlands Coalfield.

The line runs close to the north flowing River Trent, on its west side, as far as Newark, where it crosses the river. From there it traverses fairly flat land, until it reaches the important commercial centre of Lincoln, which is situated where the north flowing River Witham turns east to the North Sea and at its confluence with the Fosdyke Navigation which runs southeast. The city is of Roman origin and was built in a gap in the limestone ridge, which runs from the Cotswolds to the River Humber, gradually diminishing in height.

The route passes from Nottinghamshire into Lincolnshire between Collingham and Swinderby. Its extremities are in the respective county towns.

The branch through Southwell to Mansfield was on a rising gradient and its final few miles passed through the area of Sherwood Forest. This part was also built over red sandstones.

The maps are to the scale of 25 ins to 1 mile, with north at the top, unless otherwise indicated.

HISTORICAL BACKGROUND

The first line to reach Nottingham was that of the Midland Counties Railway from Derby and it opened on 4th June 1839. It became part of the Midland Railway in 1844. This company constructed the route between Nottingham and Lincoln, opening it on 4th August 1846. Its Act was passed in June 1845. The next line to reach Lincoln was that of the Great Northern Railway, from the south in 1848. It was extended north in 1849, when the MR opened between Mansfield and Kirkby. The GNR completed its main line north-south through Newark in 1852. The Great Central Railway was active in the extremities of our route from 1897.

The MR opened its short branch to Southwell on 1st July 1847 and extended it north to Mansfield on 3rd April 1871. The Act for the latter was passed in 1865. The route northwards came into use in 1875. The Southwell lines lost their passenger services on 12th August 1929 northwards and southwards on 13th June 1959. Total closure east of Blidworth Colliery came in 1965 and west thereof in 1983.

The MR had become part of the London Midland & Scottish Railway in 1923 and the Great Northern Railway then became a constituent of the London & North Eastern Railway. Upon nationalisation in 1948, most of the LMSR formed the London Midland Region of British Railways, while much of the LNER became its Eastern Region. However, the lines east of Carlton & Netherfield moved into the Eastern Region on 2nd April 1950. They returned to the LMR west of Newark in 1966.

The route of this album was operated by Central Trains from 2nd March 1997, following privatisation. The franchisee became East Midland on 11th November 2007, most trains originating at Cleethorpes.

NOTTINGHAM
Sneinton Jc. (Up)
CARLTON & NETHERFIELD
BURTON JOYCE
LOWDHAM
THURGARTON
BLEASBY
FISKERTON
ROLLESTON JC.
Trent Viaduct
NEWARK—
Trent Viaduct,
L.N.E.R. Level Crossing (Up)
Cottage Crossing
COLLINGHAM
SWINDERBY
THORPE-ON-THE-HILL
HYKEHAM
Boultham Crossing
LINCOLN

270 290
759
525
510 355 287
1255
L
492
L
850
L
581
L
1170
362 285
LEVEL
302
L
335
L
345 L 276

5
10
15
20
25
30

MILES FROM LONDON RD. JC.
NOTTINGHAM (ZERO)

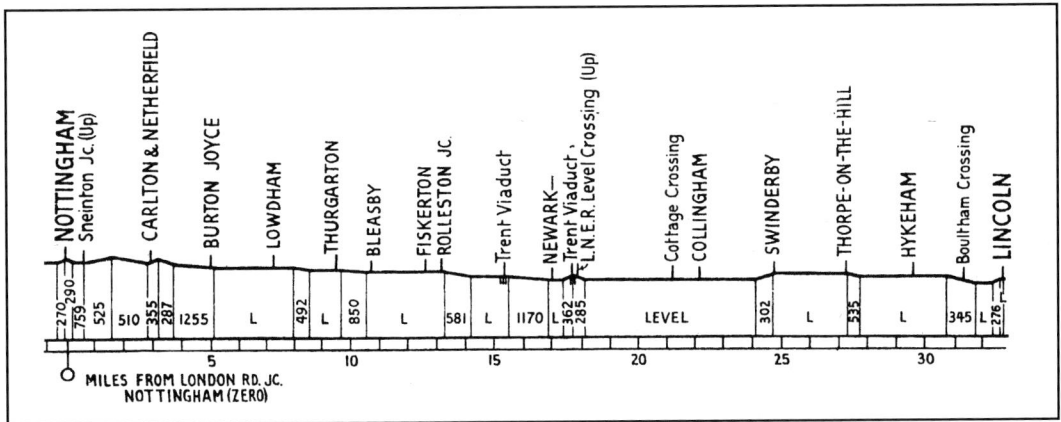

PASSENGER SERVICES

The first service between Newark and Nottingham was by steam packet on the Newark Navigation and in 1817 there were two trips per week.

The initial train service comprised five weekday trips, with two on Sundays. The figures increased to 7 and 3 in 1847. Down stopping trains from Nottingham are listed below: fast ones are in brackets.

	From Nottingham		From Newark	
	Weekdays	Sundays	Weekdays	Sundays
1846	6	2	6	2
1860	5 (1)	2 (1)	5 (1)	2 (1)
1885	7 (1)	1 (1)	8 (1)	1 (1)
1909	6 (1)	2 (1)	10 (4)	2 (1)
1935	7 (5)	3 (3)	11 (8)	3 (3)
1955	12	5	12	5
1958	21	5	12	5

The rise in 1958 was due to the advent of DMUs, but by 1987 the weekday figure was down to 13. However, while earlier most trains just ran between Lincoln and Derby, there were trains from Cleethorpes to Newark from May 1982. Sprinters of BR's provincial sector operated between Cleethorpes and Birmingham from 1987 and some fast trains were reintroduced. There were non-stop trains over the route of this album from 1989. From 1994, there were 16 weekdays trains and 8 on Sundays, the figures in 2013 being 17 and 6. Many continued to Leicester, by that time.

Southwell Branch

The first timetable showed nine trains, but this was soon reduced to one on Wednesdays only and it was horse drawn. This was withdrawn for seven years. Reopening took place on 1st September 1860 and there were soon six trains per day. (We have found no evidence of Sunday trains on the route.) By 1885, the figure was nine, 1909: 19, 1928: 23 and 1958: 19.

The section north of Southwell, through to Mansfield, had five trains in 1885, but only two were shown in 1909 and 1928, again weekdays only.

NOTTINGHAM, SOUTHWELL, NEWARK, and LINCOLN.—Midland.

Miles	Fares from Nottingham 1 cl.	Fares from Nottingham 3 cl.	Station	Week Days mrn	mrn	mrn	mrn (Fridays only)	mrn (Wednesdays only)	mrn	non	aft	aft	aft (Saturdays only)	aft	aft	aft	aft	aft (Except Saturdays)	aft (Saturdays only)	Sundays mrn	mrn	
			Station Street, Derby 363 ....dep.	3 18	5 55	7 45	9 35	1025	1025	12 0	1 20	2 20	....	4 5	5 23	7 5	8 10	9 5	1030	3 18	9 20	....
—			**Nottingham** ....dep.	3 55	7 40	8 35	1032	1110	1115	1 5	2 0	3 5	4 35	4 45	6 15	7 50	8 50	1030	1115	3 55	1010	....
3	0 6	0 3	Carlton and Gedling ...	mail	7 47	....			1122	1 12	2 9	3 14	4 42	4 52	6 22	7 57	8 58	1039	1122	mail	1017	....
5	0 8	0 5	Burton Joyce	....	7 52	....			1127	1 17	2 14	3 19	4 47	4 57	6 27	8 2	9 4	1044	1127	....	1023	....
7½	1 1	0 7½	Lowdham	....	7 58	8 48			1133	1 22	2 20	3 25	4 53	5 3	6 33	8 8	9 1)	1049	1132	....	1029	....
9½	1 4	0 9½	Thurgarton	....	8 3	8 53			1139	....	2 25	3 30	4 58	5 8	6 38	8 13	9 13			....	1035	....
11	1 6	0 11	Bleasby	....	8 7	....			1143	....	2 30	3 34	5 3	5 12	6 43	8 17	9 20			....	1040	....
12½	1 9	1 0½	Fiskerton	4 14	8 12	....			Wd	....	2 35	Sat.	5 8	5 17	6 48	8 22	Sat.			4 14	1045	....
13½	1 10	1 1	Rolleston Junction	....	8 16	9 1			1149	....	2 38	3 40	5 12	5 20	6 51	8 25	9 28			....	....	....
16	2 2	1 4	**Southwell** ... arr.	....	8 34	9 9			12 0	....	2 51	3 49	5 34	5 34	7 4	8 31	9 36			....	....	....
			Southwell ... dep.	....	....	8 40			1129	....	2 25	3 23	....	5 10	6 42	8 10	8 35			....	....	....
17	2 3	1 5	**Newark 232, 237**	4 23	8 22	9 7	1055	1133	1156	....	2 44	3 47	5 18	5 28	6 59	8 34	9 35			4 23	1054	....
22¼	3 1	1 10	Collingham	....	8 33	9 16	....	....	12 9	....	2 56	3 58		5 41	7 12	....	9 47			....	11 5	....
24¾	3 4	2 0½	Swinderby	....	8 39	9 22	....	....	1215	....	3 2	4 4		5 47	7 18	....	e			....	1111	....
27½	3 7	2 3	Thorpe-on-the-Hill	....	8 45	9 27	....	....	1221	....	3 8	4 10		5 53	7 24	....	9 56			....	1118	....
29¾	4 0	2 5½	Hykeham	....	8 51	Fri.	....	....	....	....	b	4 16		5 59	....	....	....			....	....	....
33	4 4	2 8½	**Lincoln 476, 248** ..arr.	4 50	9 0	9 37	1122	....	1235	....	3 20	4 25		6 10	7 36	....	1010			4 50	1130	....
44¾	13 5	6 6½	476 Hull (Corp. Pier) arr	7 50	....	1230	....	....	3 50	....	6 0	....		9 45	....	....	....	....	....	9 5	5 50	....

Miles	Fares from Lincoln Single	Single	Return	Return	Station	Week Days mrn	mrn	mrn	mrn	aft	mrn	aft (Weds. only)	aft (Fridays only)	aft	aft	aft	aft			Sundays aft	mail	
					Corporation Pier, Hull 476 ......dep.	....	....	6 55	....	....	9 10		1225	1225	....	4 55	....	....	....	....	4 0	....
					Lincoln ....dep.	7 0	8 15	9 40	11 0	....	1 25		3 0	3 25	5 30	8 10	....	....	....	6 35	8 10	....
3½	0 6	0 3	....	....	Hykeham	....	....	9 49	....	....	c		....	3 32	5 37	mail	....	....	....	....	....	....
5¾	0 10	0 5½	....	....	Thorpe-on-the-Hill	7 10	....	9 55	1110	....	1 36		....	3 38	5 43	....	....	....	....	6 47	....	....
8	1 1	0 8	....	....	Swinderby	7 16	....	10 0	1116	....	1 42		....	3 44	5 48	....	....	....	....	6 53	....	....
10¾	1 6	0 10½	....	....	Collingham	7 22	8 32	10 6	1122	....	1 48		....	3 50	5 54	8 27	....	....	....	6 59	8 27	....
16	2 2	1 3½	....	....	**Newark 237, 232**	7 33	8 40	1015	1132	....	1 59	2 30	3 22	4 0	6 2	8 38	9 5	....	....	7 9	8 38	....
22	2 11	1 10	....	....	**Southwell** ... arr.	8 34	9 9	1033	12 0	....	2 18	2 51		4 21	6 23	9 33	9 36	....	....	....	....	....
					Southwell ... dep.	7 30	8 40	1011	1129	....	1 58	2 25		3 53	6 0	8 35	8 35	....	....	....	....	....
19½	2 8	1 7½	....	....	Rolleston Junction	7 41	8 49	1023	1139	....	2 6	2 36		4 10	6 12	8 46	9 13	....	....	....	....	....
20½	2 9	1 8	....	....	Fiskerton	7 44	8 53	c	....	....	2 11	....		4 15	6 15	....	9 17	....	....	7 20	8 47	....
22	2 11	1 9½	....	....	Bleasby	7 48	8 57	c	W S	....	2 15	....		4 19	6 19	....	9 22	....	....	7 25	....	....
23½	3 2	1 11	....	....	Thurgarton	7 52	9 1	1033	1147	....	2 19	....		4 22	6 23	....	9 27	....	....	7 30	....	....
25½	3 5	2 1	....	....	Lowdham	7 58	9 5	1037	1152	2 10	2 25	....		4 28	6 29	....	9 33	....	....	7 36	....	....
28	3 8	2 3½	....	....	Burton Joyce	8 5	9 13	c d	1158	2 16	2 31	....		4 36	6 36	....	9 40	....	....	7 42	....	....
30	4 0	2 5½	....	....	Carlton and Gedling....	8 10	9 17	c	12 2	2 20	2 35	2 52	3 41	4 40	6 41	9 2	9 45	....	....	7 49	9 2	....
33	4 4	2 8½	....	....	**Nottingham 375** ...arr.	8 19	9 25	1050	1210	2 28	2 43	3 0	3 50	4 50	6 50	9 12	9 55	....	....	7 58	9 10	....
49	6 1	3 8½	....	....	Derby 363 ....arr.	9 18	1015	1145	1252	....	3 35	3 35	4 35	5 30	7 48	9 48	1120	....	....	9 40	9 48	....

b Stops when required to set down from London. **c** Stop when required to take up for London. **d** Stops on Wednesdays and Saturdays. **e** Stops on Saturdays; and other days when required to set down from Nottingham, and North and South thereof: also to take up for Lincoln.

December 1895

March 1909

MANSFIELD, SOUTHWELL, and NEWARK.—Midland.

Miles	Station	Week Days mrn	mrn	mrn	mrn	mrn	mrn	mrn (Weds. only)	mrn (Thurs. only)	mrn	aft	aft	aft	aft	aft	aft	aft	aft	aft	aft	aft	aft	aft	aft (Sats. only)
	Mansfield ....dep.	....	....	....	....	9 38	....		1025	....	....	....	....	3 35	....	....	....	6h17	....	....	....	8s45	....	
4¾	Blidworth and Rainworth	....	....	....	....	9 46	....		1033	....	....	....	....	3 43	....	....	....	6h25	....	....	....	8s53	....	
7¾	Farnsfield	....	....	....	....	9 53	....		1040	....	....	....	3b30	3 50	....	....	....	6h32	....	....	....	9s0	....	
10	Kirklington........	....	....	....	....	9 58	....		1045	....	....	....	3b36	3 55	....	....	....	6h37	....	....	....	9s5	....	
12½	**Southwell**	7 20	7 47	8 38	9 38	10 5	1050	•	1050	1150	1 30	2 24	3 50	4 1	5 8	6 0	6 33	6 57	7 19	8 10	8 35	9s12	9 28	1140
15	Rolleston Junction 583 arr.	7 26	7 53	8 44	9 44	1011	1057		1057	1156	1 36	2 30	3 56	4 7	5 14	6 6	6 39	7 3	7 25	8 16	8 41	9s18	9 34	1146
	Rolleston Junction 583 dep.	7 27	7 56	8 45	....	1020	....	1142	12 3	12 3	1 41	2 40	....	4 9	5 21	....	6 47	7 8	....	8 21	....	....	9 54	1155
18½	**Newark** ** 345, 583..arr.	7 34	8 4	8 52	....	1027	....	1149	1211	1211	1 48	2 50	....	4 16	5 30	....	6 54	7 16	....	8 29	....	....	10 2	12 3
34½	583 Lincoln ....arr.	....	8 39	9 53	....	1143	....	....	1246	1246	....	3 26	....	5 4	6 6	....	....	7 52	....	9s0	....	t	1028	1232

Miles	Station	Week Days mrn	mrn	mrn	mrn	mrn	mrn	mrn (Thurs. only)	aft	aft	aft	aft (Weds. only)	aft	aft	aft	aft	aft	aft	aft	aft	aft	aft (Sats. only)	
	583 Lincoln ....dep.	....	6 50	6 50	8 5	9 2	1020	1020	....	1 0	....	....	3 25	3 25	5 28	....	....	....	....	8 10	9s15	....	....
—	**Newark** ....dep.	....	8 0	8 15	9 0	9 38	1054	1054	....	1 37	....	2 30	4 2	5 10	6 3	....	....	7 18	....	8 37	9v30	....	....
3½	Rolleston Junction. arr.	....	8 8	8 23	9 7	9 47	11 2	11 2	....	1 45	....	2 38	4 11	5 17	6 12	....	....	7 26	....	8 46	9 38	....	....
	Rolleston Junction. dep.	7 4	8 10	8 24	9 11	9 52	11 5	11 5	12 6	1 50	2 42	2 42	4 23	5 24	6 18	6 48	7 9	7 30	8 23	8 50	10 0	1157	....
6	**Southwell**........	7 11	8 16	8 30	9 17	9 58	1111	1111	1212	1 56	2 48	2 48	4 29	5 30	6 24	6 54	7 15	7 36	8 29	8 56	10 6	12 3	....
8½	Kirklington........	....	....	8 36	....	....	....	1119	....	....	....	2 55	....	5 36	....	....	7h22	....	....	....	....		....
10¾	Farnsfield	....	....	8 42	....	....	....	1125	....	....	....	3 1	....	5 42	....	....	7h28	....	....	....	....		....
13¾	Blidworth and Rainworth	....	....	8 50	....	....	....	1132	....	....	....	....	....	5 50	....	....	7h36	....	....	....	....		....
18½	**Mansfield 575, 577, 591** ar	....	....	9 0	....	....	....	1142	....	....	....	....	....	6 0	....	....	7h46	....	....	....	....		....

NOTES.

b Wednesdays only.
h Thursdays only.
s Saturdays only.
t Arrives at 10 38 aft. on Saturdays.
v Leaves at 9 50 aft. on Saturdays.
** About 1 mile to G. N. Station.

NOTTINGHAM, NEWARK, and LINCOLN.—Midland.

Miles	Down.	Week Days ngt.	mrn	mrn	mrn	mrn	mrn	mrn (Weds. only)	mrn	mrn (Except Saturdays)	mrn	mrn	aft (Wednesdays & Saturdays)	aft	aft	aft	aft	aft	aft	aft (Except Saturdays)	aft (Saturdays only)	aft (Except Thursdays and Saturdays)	aft (Thursdays & Saturdays)	ngt. (Saturdays only)		Sundays	ngt.	mrn	aft
	St. Pancras Station, 530 London ....dep.	12 0	....	....	....	5 0	8 0	....	....	9 30	1025	....	....	....	12 0	2 5	3 0	....	4 55	5 42	5 42	7 25	7h25	....	....	Sat.	12c0	....	4 0
	553 Manchester (Cen.).. "	12b55	....	....	....	....	8 32	....	9 20	1020	1020	1057	....	....	1220	1 50	....	4 20	....	5 50	5 50	7 25	7 25	....	....	Sat.	12c5	....	5 25
	587 Derby 592........ "	3 18	4 50	5 50	5 50	7 40	9 57	1020	1055	12 6	12 6	1 15	....	....	2 18	4 2	5 15	5 45	7 2	8 34	8 34	9 40	1045	....	....	mrn	3 18	9 12	7 10
—	**Nottingham**........dep.	3 55	6 0	6 30	7 20	8 35	1058	1115	1125	1245	1 5	1 50	....	2 5	3 42	4 45	6 10	6 40	7 45	9 20	9 20	1038	1120	....	....	....	3 55	10 5	8 10
3	Carlton and Netherfield *....	....	6 7	6 37	7 27	8 42	....	....	1134	1252	1 12	1 57	....	2 12	3 49	4 52	6 17	6 47	7 52	9 27	9 27	1045	1127	....	....	....	mrn	1012	8 17
5	Burton Joyce........	....	6 13	6 43	7 33	8 48	....	....	1140	1258	1 18	2 3	....	2 18	3 55	4 58	6 23	6 53	7 58	9 33	9 33	1051	1133	....	...	....	....	1018	8 23
7½	Lowdham........	....	6 19	6 49	7 39	8 54	....	1128	1146	1 3	1 24	2 8	2 9	2 24	4 1	5 4	6 29	6 59	8 4	9 39	9 39	1056	1139	....	....	....	....	1024	8 29
9½	Thurgarton........	....	....	....	7 44	8 59	....	1132	1151		1 29		2 14	2 29	4 6	5 9	6 34	....	8 9	9 44	9 44		1144	....	....	....	....	1029	8 34
11	Bleasby	....	....	....	7 48	9 3	....	1137	1155		1 33	....	2 18	2 33	4 10	5 13	6 38	a	8 13	9 48	9 48		1148	....	....	....	....	1033	8 38
12½	Fiskerton	4 14	....	....	7 53	9 8	....	....	12 0		1 38	....	2 23	2 38	4 16	5 18	6 43	....	8 18	t	9 53		1153	....	....	....	4 14	1038	8 43
13½	Rolleston Junction 582........	....	....	....	7 56	9 10	....	1142	12 3		1 41	....	2 26	2 40	4 19	5 21	6 47	7 8	8 21	9 54	9 56		Sat.	....	....	....	....	....	....
16	582 **Southwell** ...... arr.	....	....	....	8 16	9 17	....	....	1212		1 56	....	....	2 48	4 29	5 30	6 54	7 15	8 29	10 6	10 6		12s3	....	....	....	....	....	....
	582 **Southwell** ...... dep.	....	....	....	7 47	8 38	10 5	1050	1150		1 30	....	....	2 24	4 1	5 8	6 33	6 57	8 10	9 28	9 28		1140	....	....	....	....	....	....
17	**Newark** † 338, 345	4 23	6 31	....	8 4	9 18	1121	1149	1211		1 48	....	2 33	2 50	4 28	5 30	6 54	7 16	8 29	10 2	10 4		12 3	12 4	....	....	4 23	1045	8 51
22¼	Collingham........	....	....	....	8 13	9 28	....		1220		....	....	....	3 0	4 38	5 40	....	7 26	8s43	1012	1014		....	1214	....	....	....	1055	9 0
24¾	Swinderby	....	....	....	8 19	9 34	....		1226		....	....	....	3 6	4 44	5 46	....	7 32	....	....	1020		....	....	....	....	....	11 1	9 6
27½	Thorpe-on-the-Hill	....	....	....	8 25	9 40	....		1232		....	....	....	3 12	4 50	5 52	....	7 38	....	....	1026		....	....	....	....	....	11 7	9 12
29¾	Hykeham........ [702, 711	....	....	....	8 32	9 46	....		1238		....	....	....	3 17	4 56	5 57	....	7 44	....	....	1032		....	....	....	....	....	1112	9 18
33	**Lincoln 365, 376, 384,** arr.	4 48	....	....	8 39	9 53	1143	•	1246		....	....	....	3 26	5 4	6 6	....	7 52	9s0	1028	1038		....	1232	....	....	4 48	1121	9 26

Mls	Up.	Week Days mrn	mrn	mrn	mrn	mrn	mrn	mrn	aft (Except Saturdays)	aft	aft	aft (Weds. only)	aft (Fridays only)	aft	aft	aft	aft	aft	aft (Sats. only)	aft (Except Saturdays)	aft (Saturdays only)	aft (Except Thursdays and Saturdays)			Sundays mrn	aft	aft	
—	**Lincoln**........dep.	....	6 50	....	8 5	9 2	9 45	1020		1 0	....	....	2 50	3 25	....	5 28	....	8 10		....	9 15		....	....	1145	6 5	8 10	....
3½	Hykeham........	....	6 57	....	8 12	9 9	....	1027		1 7	....	....	....	3 34	....	5 35	....	....		....	9 22		....	....	1152	6 12	....	....
5¾	Thorpe-on-the-Hill........	....	7 3	....	8 18	9 15	....	1033		1 13	....	....	....	3 40	....	5 41	....	....		....	9 28		....	....	1158	6 18	....	....
8¼	Swinderby........	....	7 9	....	8 24	9 21	....	1039		1 19	....	....	....	3 46	....	5 47	....	....		....	9 34		....	....	12 4	6 24	....	....
10¾	Collingham........	....	7 15	....	8 30	9 27	....	1045		1 25	....	....	....	3 52	....	5 53	....	8 27		....	9 40		....	....	1210	6 30	8 27	....
16	**Newark** † 338, 345	....	7 25	8 0	8 40	9 38	10 8	1054		1 37	2d10	2 30	3 12	4 2	4 15	6 37	7 18	8 37		9 30	9 50		....	....	1219	6 39	8 37	....
22	582 **Southwell** ...... arr.	....	8 16	8 16	9 17	9 58	....	1111		1 56	....	2 48	....	4 29	....	6 24	7 36	8 56	....	10 6	10 6		....	....	....	....	....	....
	582 **Southwell** ...... dep.	....	7 20	7 47	8 38	9 38	10 5	1050		1 30	....	2 24	....	4 1	4 1	6 0	7 19	8 35	9 12	9 28	9 28		....	....	....	....	....	....
19½	Rolleston Junction 582	....	7 33	8 8	8 48	9 47	1016	11 2		1 45	....	2 38	....	4 11	4 23	6 12	7 26	8 46	9 25	9 38	9 58		....	....	....	....	....	....
20½	Fiskerton........	....	7 37	8 11	8 51	9 51	....	11 6		1 49	....		....	....	4 26	6 15	7 30	....	9 28	9 41	10 1		....	....	1227	6 47	8 46	....
22	Bleasby	....	7 42	8 16	8 56	9 56	....	1111		1 54	....		....	....	4 31	6 20	7 35	....	9 33	9 46	10 6		....	....	1230	6 50	....	....
23½	Thurgarton........	....	7 46	8 20	9 0	10 0	....	1115		1 58	....		....	....	4 35	6 24	7 39	....	9 37	9 50	1010		....	....	1236	6 55	....	....
25½	Lowdham........	7 0	7 51	8 25	9 5	10 5	....	1119	1 35	2 4	2 23		3 25	4 22	4 40	6 29	7 44	....	9 42	9 55	1015	1112	....	....	1241	6 59	....	....
28	Burton Joyce........	7 6	7 58	8 31	9 11	1011	....	1126	1 41	2 10	2 29		....	....	4 46	6 35	7 50	....	9 48	10 1	1021	....	....	....	1247	7 4	....	....
30	Carlton and Netherfield *....	7 13	8 6	8 38	9 18	1017	....	1132	1 48	2 17	2 35		....	4 32	4 53	6 42	7 56	9 2	9 55	10 7	1028	1124	....	....	1253	7 12	9 2	....
33	**Nottingham 541, 586**...arr.	7 22	8 16	8 45	9 25	1024	1034	1142	1 55	2 24	2 42	2 57	3 40	4 40	5 0	6 49	8 4	9 10	10 2	1014	1035	1130	....	....	1 0	7 19	9 9	....
49	586 Derby 592........arr.	8 36	9 9	9 30	1020	....	1148	1230	3 5	....	3 20	4 9	4 45	5 21	6 0	7 37	9 0	9 47	....	1135	1135	1234	....	....	1 52	8 58	9 47	....
110½	550 Manchester (Cen.).. "	9 52	....	1115	1220	....	1242	2 38	....		5 20	6 20	6 20	7 15	8 40	1011	1035	2h38	....	2 38	3 10	2 38	....	....	4 25	1047	5 20	....
159½	541 London (St. Pancras). "	....	1040	12 5	....	....	1 14	3 7	....		5 21	6 30	6 30	7 41	8 10	10 0	1113	4 20	....	4 20	4 20	4 20	....	....	4 22	10 5	4 20	....

a Stops to set down from Manchester and beyond.
b Except Monday mornings.
c Saturday night times.
d Wednesdays and Saturdays.
h Except Sunday mornings.
n Leaves at 6 30 aft. on Saturdays.
s Saturdays only.
t Sets down when required.
* Station for Gedling and Colwick.
† About 1 mile to G. N. Station.

March 1909

MANSFIELD, SOUTHWELL, and NEWARK.—Midland.

Mls		mrn	mrn	mrn Thursdays.	mrn Except Thurs.	aft Sats. only.	aft	aft	aft Thursdays.
—	**Mansfield** ....dep.	....	9 45	11 0			....	3 20	6 15
4¾	Blidworth&Rainworth	....	9 54	1110			....	3 31	6 24
7¾	Farnsfield	....	10 1	1117			3c10	3 39	6 31
10	Kirklington&Edingley	....	10 6	1123			3c16	3 46	6 36
12½	**Southwell**...........	7 30	1011	1129	1129		3 23	3 53	6 42
15	Rolleston *(above)*..arr.	7 36	1018	1135	1135	2 28	3 29	3 59	6 48
—	NOTTINGHAM..arr.	8 19	1050	1210	1210	....	4 50	4 50	9 12
18½	**Newark 237**......arr.	7 45	1028	1156	1156	2 35	3 47	4 8	6 59
—	LINCOLN ......arr.	9 0	11b5	1235	1235	....	4 25	6 10	7 36

	mrn	mrn Except Thurs.	mrn Thursdays.	aft	aft	aft Thursdays.
LINCOLN ......dep.	7 0	11 0	11 0	....	3 25	....
Newark ....dep.	8 20	1132	1132	2c30	5 10	....
NOTTINGHAM..dep.	7 40	1115	1115	2c0	4 45	6 15
Rolleston.........dep.	8 29	1154	1154	2c45	5 26	6 58
Southwell...........	8 34	12 0	12 0	2c51	5 34	7 4
Kirklington&Edingley	8 42		12 7	2c58	5 42	7 11
Farnsfield [Rainworth	8 48		1213	3c5	5 48	7 17
Blidworth and [389	8 55		1221	....	5 56	7 24
Mansfield 386, 387, ar	9 7		1233	....	6 10	7 35

b Arrives on Fridays only. **c** Wednesdays only.

December 1895

SOUTHWELL, ROLLESTON JUNCTION, and NEWARK
One class only between Southwell and Rolleston Junction

Week Days only (mrn / aft)

Miles	HOUR	7	7	8	8	9	9	10	11	12	1	2	2	2	3	4	4	5	5	6	6	7	7	7	8	9	E 9	9	S 9	S 11
—	**Southwell** ....dep.	20	45	30	54	26	52	55	47	47	30	0	20	47	45	7	37	11	40	17	41	5	25	52	23	25	.	47	.	17
	Rolleston Junction 700 arr.	25	50	35	59	31	57	**0**	52	52	35	5	25	52	50	12	42	16	45	22	46	10	30	57	28	30	.	52	.	22
2½	Rolleston Junction 700 dep.	.	58	36	**8**	41	**0**	9	**0**		**2**	19	29	**4**	.	.	50	24	57	.	53	14	.	**4**	.	.	54	.	59	29
6	Newark C700, 310 arr.	.	**8**	43	15	50	7	18	8	.	10	26	38	11	.	.	58	31	**5**	.	**0**	24	.	12	.	.	**3**	.	**3**	38

Week Days only (mrn / aft)

Miles	HOUR	7	7	9	9	10	10	12	12	1	2	2	2	3	4	4	5	5	6	6	7	7	8	8	9	E 9	S 10	S 11
—	**Newark** ....dep.	22	54	8	28	25	59	.	47	33	.	.	48	47	10	.	.	50	22	.	.	27	.	26	27	.	.	.
	Rolleston Junction arr	30	**2**	15	36	32	**8**	.	56	42	.	.	56	56	17	.	.	58	31	.	.	35	.	35	36	.	.	.
3½	Rolleston Junction dep.	33	5	16	42	33	13	2	**0**	45	11	32	**7**	58	20	51	26	**0**	33	55	17	38	10	37	38	55	2	32
6	**Southwell** 700 .....arr.	38	10	21	47	38	18	7	5	50	16	37	12	**3**	25	56	31	5	38	**0**	22	43	15	42	43	**0**	7	37

B About ½ mile to L. & N. E. Central and over ½ mile to Market Place Stations **C** About 1 mile to L & N. E.
D Over 1 mile to Friargate Station **E** Except Sats **H** Arr 6 24 aft **K** About ¼ mile to Victoria Station
L Arr 4 17 aft **P** Arr 8 45 mrn **R** One class only, except on Sats **S** or S Sats only
T Arr Duffield at 7 47, and Hazelwood at 7 58 aft **V** Fris and Sats **X** Stops at 8 27 mrn to set down * mrn † aft
OTHER TRAINS between Rolleston Junction and Newark, page 700

Where the MINUTES under the Hours change to a LOWER figure and DARKER type it indicates the NEXT HOUR

January 1935

NOTTINGHAM, SOUTHWELL, NEWARK, and LINCOLN

Miles from Nottingham	Down	Week Days ngt.	mn	mrn	mn	mrn	mrn	mrn	mrn S	mrn	mrn	mrn	aft	aft E	aft	aft	aft	aft	aft Z	aft	aft S	aft	aft	Sundays Sat ngt.	mrn	mrn	mrn		aft	aft			
	642 **London** (St Pan)..dep.	12z5	..	..	225	4 25	..	9 0	..	10 0	11 0	..	..	..	2 0	2 0	..	3 30	3 30	5 0	615	6 15	6 25	..	..	..	1010	..	5 0	6 30	..	..	..
	660 BRISTOL (T M) .... "	7 20	..	1010	..	..	..	..	7 52	9 5	9 5	9 5	..	..	1235	1235	12 35	2 20	2 20	..	5 0	5 0	..	7 20	1 10	..	8 50	..	2 0	..	..	..	..
	660 BOURNEMOUTH W. "	3§45	..	..	..	..	..	..	..	..	..	..	..	..	..	1030	10 30	1140	1140	..	..	..	..	3 45	..	..	..	..	..	..	..	..	..
	660 BIRMINGHAM (N St) "	1055	..	4016	..	6 55	8J40	8 45	1013	1140	1140	1140	..	..	2 37	3 4	3 4	4 30	4g55	..	7 5	7 5	8§20	1055	7 20	10g22	1220	..	425	8g45	..	..	..
	667 MANCHESTER (Cen) "	12X0	..	..	..	..	7 20	8 55	9 45	9 45	9 45	..	..	..	1 45	1 45	..	3 25	4E35	4Z35	550	5 50	7 25	12 0	..	..	9 12	..	520	..	..	..	..
—	**Nottingham** ....dep.	4 0	6 0	7 23	822	9 10	1050	1125	1215	1 28	1 45	2 10	230	..	4 28	4 50	5 23	6 19	6 55	7 30	850	9F20	10 55	4 0	1010	12 17	2 25	..	830	10 6	..	..	..
3	Carlton and Netherfield **A**	mrn	..	7 31	829	9 17	..	1133	1222	1 35	1 52	..	237	..	..	4 57	5 30	6 26	..	7 37	857	9F27	11 2	mrn	1017	..	2 32	..	837	..	..	..	..
5	Burton Joyce............	..	..	7 36	834	9 22	..	1138	1227	1 40	1 57	..	242	..	..	5 2	5 35	6 31	..	7 42	9 2	9F32	11 7	..	1022	..	2 37	..	842	..	..	..	..
7½	Lowdham..............	..	612	7 41	839	9 27	..	1143	1232	1 45	2 2	..	247	..	4 40	5 7	5 40	6 36	..	7 47	9 7	9F37	11 12	..	1027	..	2 42	..	847	..	..	..	..
9½	Thurgarton............	..	..	7 46	844	9 32	..	1148	1237	1 50	2 7	..	252	..	..	5 12	5 45	6 41	..	7 52	912	9F42	11T17	..	1032	..	2 47	..	852	..	..	..	..
11	Bleasby	..	..	7 50	848	9 36	..	1152	1241	1 54	2 11	..	256	..	..	5 16	5 49	6 45	..	7 56	916	9F46	11T21	..	1036	..	2 51	..	856	..	..	..	..
12¼	Fiskerton	4 19	..	7 54	852	..	..	1156	1245	1 58	2 15	..	3 0	..	..	5 20	5 53	6 49	..	8 0	920	9F50	11T25	4 19	1040	..	2 55	..	9 0	..	..	..	..
13¾	Rolleston Junction 701...	..	..	7 58	856	9 41	11 9	12 0	1249	2 2	2 19	2 29	3 4	..	4 50	5 24	5 57	6 53	7 14	8 4	924	9F54	11T29	..	..	..	..	..	..	..	..	..	..
16	701 **Southwell F** ... arr.	..	..	8 10	921	9 47	1118	12 7	1 5	2 16	2 37	2 37	312	..	4 56	5 31	6 5	7 0	7 22	8 15	943	10F0	11S37	..	..	..	..	..	..	..	..	..	..
	701 **Southwell F** ... dep.	..	..	7 45	..	9 26	1055	1147	..	1 30	2 0	2 20	247	..	4 37	5 11	5 40	6 41	7 5	7 52	..	9§25	11S17	..	..	..	..	..	..	..	..	..	..
17	**Newark B** 810, 817	4 28	627	8 8	9 4	9 50	1118	12 8	1256	2 10	2 26	2 38	311	..	4 58	5 31	6 5	7 0	7 24	8 12	931	10F3	11T37	4 30	1050	12 44	3 5	..	910	1112	..	..	..
22¼	Collingham.............	..	..	8 17	..	9 59	..	1216	..	2 19	..	2 47	..	.	5 7	..	6 14	..	..	8 21	F	1012	11S47	..	1059	..	3 14	..	919	..	..	..	..
24¼	Swinderby.............	..	..	8 23	..	10 5	..	1222	..	2 25	..	2 53	..	..	5 13	..	6 20	..	..	8 27	S	1023	..	..	11 5	..	3 20	..	925	..	..	..	..
27¼	Thorpe-on-the-Hill	..	..	8 28	..	1010	..	1227	..	2 30	..	2 58	..	4 55	5 18	..	6 25	..	..	8 32	S	1028	..	..	1110	..	3 25	..	930	..	..	..	..
29¾	Hykeham .....[**910, 918**	..	..	8 34	..	1016	..	1234	..	2 37	..	3 5	..	5 10	5 25	..	6 32	..	..	8 39	S	1034	11S58	..	1117	..	3 32	..	937	..	..	..	..
33	**Lincoln** (Mid) 887, 892 arr	4 50	..	8 40	..	1022	1140	1240	..	2 43	..	3 11	..	5 15	5 31	..	6 38	..	7 46	8 45	U	1028	12S4	4 54	1123	1 5	3 38	..	943	1134	..	..	..

Miles	Up	Week Days mrn	mrn	mrn	mrn Y	mn	mrn	mrn D		aft	aft S	aft	aft	aft	aft	aft	aft	aft	aft	aft	aft		Sundays mrn		aft	aft		aft	aft		aft		
—	**Lincoln** (Mid).........dep.	..	6 55	7 20	8 30	..	9 24	1025	..	1225	..	1 0	..	3 15	4E35	5 7	..	5 50	..	8 0	8 55	..	1035	..	12 5	4 45	..	7 20	7 45	..	8 0	..	..
3½	Hykeham...............	..	7 2	7 27	..	..	9 31	1032	..	..	..	1 7	..	3 22	4E42	5 14	..	5 57	..	..	9 2	..	..	..	1212	4 52	..	7 27	..	..	..	..	..
5¾	Thorpe-on-the-Hill.......	..	..	7 33	..	..	..	1038	..	..	..	1 13	..	3 28	4E47	5 20	..	6 3	..	..	9 8	..	..	..	1218	4 58	..	7 33	..	..	..	..	..
8½	Swinderby..............	..	..	7 39	..	..	..	1044	..	..	..	1 18	..	3 33	Stop	5 25	..	6 8	..	..	9 13	..	..	..	1223	5 3	..	7 38	..	..	..	..	..
10¾	Collingham.............	..	7 14	7 45	8 45	..	9 42	1050	..	..	..	1 24	..	3 39	aft	5 31	..	6 14	..	8 16	9 19	..	..	..	1229	5 9	..	7 44	..	..	816	..	..
16	**Newark B** 810, 817	6 45	7 22	7 54	8 55	928	9 50	1059	..	1247	1 12	1 33	2 48	3 47	4 10	5 39	550	6 22	7 27	8 26	9 27	..	1057	..	1238	5 18	..	7 52	8 7	..	826	..	..
↔	701 **Southwell F** ... arr.	..	7 38	8 10	9 21	947	1038	1118	..	1 5	..	1 50	3 12	4 3	4 25	6 5	6 5	6 38	7 43	8 42	9 43	..	..	..	..	..	..	..	..	..	..	..	..
	701 **Southwell F** ... dep.	..	7 20	7 45	8 54	926	9 52	1055	..	1247	1247	1 30	2 47	3 45	4 7	5 40	540	6 17	7 25	8 23	9 25	..	..	..	..	..	..	..	..	..	..	..	..
19½	Rolleston Junction 701...	..	7 30	8 2	9 3	936	9 59	11 8	..	1256	1 20	1 42	2 56	3 56	4 18	5 48	558	6 31	7 35	8 35	9 36	..	..	..	..	..	..	..	..	..	..	..	..
20¾	Fiskerton	6 54	7 33	8 5	..	940	..	1111	..	..	..	1 46	..	..	4 21	..	6 1	..	7 38	..	9 39	..	..	..	1247	5 28	..	8 1	..	..	835	..	..
22	Bleasby................	6 58	7 37	8 10	..	944	..	1116	..	..	1 26	1 50	..	..	4 25	..	6 5	..	7 42	..	9 43	..	..	..	1251	5 32	..	8 5	..	..	..	..	..
23½	Thurgarton.............	7 2	7 41	8 14	..	948	..	1120	..	..	1 30	1 54	3 2	..	4 29	..	6 9	..	7 46	..	9 47	..	..	..	1255	5 36	..	8 9	..	..	..	..	..
25½	Lowdham..............	7 7	7 46	8 19	..	953	..	1125	..	..	1 35	1 59	3 7	..	4 34	..	614	..	7 51	..	9 52	..	..	..	1 0	5 41	..	8 14	..	..	..	..	..
28	Burton Joyce...........	7 12	7 51	8 25	..	958	..	1131	..	..	1 40	2 4	3 12	..	4 39	..	619	..	7 56	..	9 57	..	..	..	1 5	5 46	..	8 19	..	..	..	..	..
30	Carlton and Netherfield **A**	7 17	7 56	8 31	..	103	..	1137	..	..	1 45	2 9	3 17	..	4 45	..	625	..	8 2	..	10 2	..	..	..	1 10	5 51	..	8 24	..	..	..	..	..
33	**Nottingham 649, 680** arr	7 23	8 2	8 37	9 20	109	1018	1143	..	1 15	1 51	2 15	3 23	4 16	4 51	6 6	631	6 50	8 8	8 55	10 8	..	1123	..	1 16	5 57	..	8 30	8 44	..	855	..	..
110¼	664 MANCHESTER (Cen) arr.	9E52	..	1134	..	..	1254	2 40	..	..	..	4 23	6a23	6a23	..	8 51	..	..	1030	5 20	5 20	..	..	..	4 11	1055	..	..	..	..	550	..	..
90	656 BIRMINGHAM (N St) "	9 16	1016	..	11g8	..	1 4	1 33	..	..	..	3 49	5 32	6 19	8 7	8 7	8 7	8 57	1010	11S31	2 5	..	1g25	..	4 0	8 44	..	g	1057	..	..	..	..
257½	656 BOURNEMOUTH W.. "	..	..	..	4 35	..	..	7 14	..	..	..	1018	..	..	..	..	..	..	..	‡	1051	..	..	..	..	..	..	..	..	..	..	..	..
178¼	656 BRISTOL (T M) .... "	1140	..	..	1 25	..	..	3 32	..	..	..	€ 5	7 38	1026	..	..	..	1220	..	..	5 50	..	..	..	6 36	1220	..	..	..	..	..	..	..
159¼	649 **London** (St Pan).. "	..	1043	..	12 8	..	1 15	3 26	..	3 47	..	5 36	6 35	7 55	7 55	..	9 2	..	..	4 33	4 33	..	2 32	..	5 0	8 55	..	1121	4 55	..	..	..	..

A Station for Gedling & Colwick. About 1 ml to Gedling & Carlton Sta. *a* Arr 6 48 aft Sats. **B** About 1 mile to L & N E Sta. B Except Suns.
D Thro Train. Lincoln to Leicester and Birmingham. D Except Mons. **E** or E Except Sats. **F** One class only between Rolleston Junc & Southwell.
F 5 mins. later on Sats. *g* Via Leicester. J Dep 7 50 mrn Sats. **S** or S Sats only. T Thurs & Sats
U Arr. 10 40 aft. Sats. X Dep 10 40 aft Suns. **Y Through Express**, Lincoln to Birmingham. Thro Carrs, Lincoln to Bristol.
Z Through Express, Birmingham to Lincoln. Thro Carrs, Bristol to Lincoln. Z Dep 4 25 aft Sats. *z* Mons only.
‡ Except Sun mrns. § Dep. 9 47 aft. Sats.

Extra.—On Week-days Nottingham to Lowdham at 12 55, 5E55, and 6 28 aft., returning at 1 51 and 8 20 aft. calling at Carlton and Netherfield and Burton Joyce.

January 1935

SOUTHWELL, ROLLESTON JUNCTION and NEWARK
Second Class only between Southwell and Rolleston Junction

Week Days only

Miles		a.m	a.m	a.m	a.m	a.m	a.m	a.m S	p.m S	p.m S	p.m S	p.m	p.m	p.m E	p.m S	p.m	pm	p.m	p.m E	p.m	p.m	p.m	p.m	p.m
—	**Southwell**......... dep	6 33	7 27	7 50	8 32	8 55	1015	11 0	1215	1240	1 10	1 30	2 15	3 15	3 20	4 10	434	5 20	5 50	6 15	6 34	7 25	8 30	9 20
	Rolleston Junction arr	6 38	7 32	7 55	8 37	9 0	1020	11 5	1220	1245	1 15	1 35	2 20	3 20	3 25	4 15	439	5 25	5 55	6 2[illegible]	6 39	7 30	8 35	9 25
	Rolleston Junction dep	6 57	..	7 57	8E50	9 24	1022	11 9	1222	1247	1 22	..	2 22	3 22	3 32	4 22	..	5 29	6 3	6 22	6 52	7 32	8 46	9 27
	Newark (Castle).... arr	7 3	..	8 3	8E58	9 31	1028	1118	1228	1255	1 28	..	2 28	3 28	3 38	4 28	..	5 35	6 11	6 30	7 0	7 38	8 55	9 33

Week Days only

Miles		a.m	a.m	a.m	a.m	a.m S	p.m E	a.m	a.m S	a.m S	p.m S	p.m S	p.m	p.m	p.m	p.m	p.m	pm	p.m E	p.m	p.m	p.m	p.m	p.m S
—	**Newark** (Castle) ... dep	6 35	7 30	7 52	8 35	8 55	9 15	1035	..	1135	1248	1 10	1 35	2 35	3 35	4E10	4B37	..	5 35	..	6 35	7 33	8 40	..
	Rolleston Junction arr	6 41	7 36	8 0	8 41	9 3	9 22	1041	..	1141	1256	1 17	1 41	2 41	3 41	4E17	4B43	..	5 41	..	6 41	7 39	8 46	..
3¾	**Rolleston Junction** dep	7 0	7 40	8 4	8 45	9 30	9 30	1045	1115	1225	1 0	1 20	1 45	2 45	3 45	4 25	4 50	535	6 5	6 25	6 45	7 45	8 50	9 30
6¼	**Southwell** .... arr	7 5	7 45	8 9	8 50	9 35	9 35	1050	1120	1230	1 5	1 25	1 50	2 50	3 50	4 30	4 55	540	6 10	6 30	6 50	7 50	8 55	9 35

June 1958

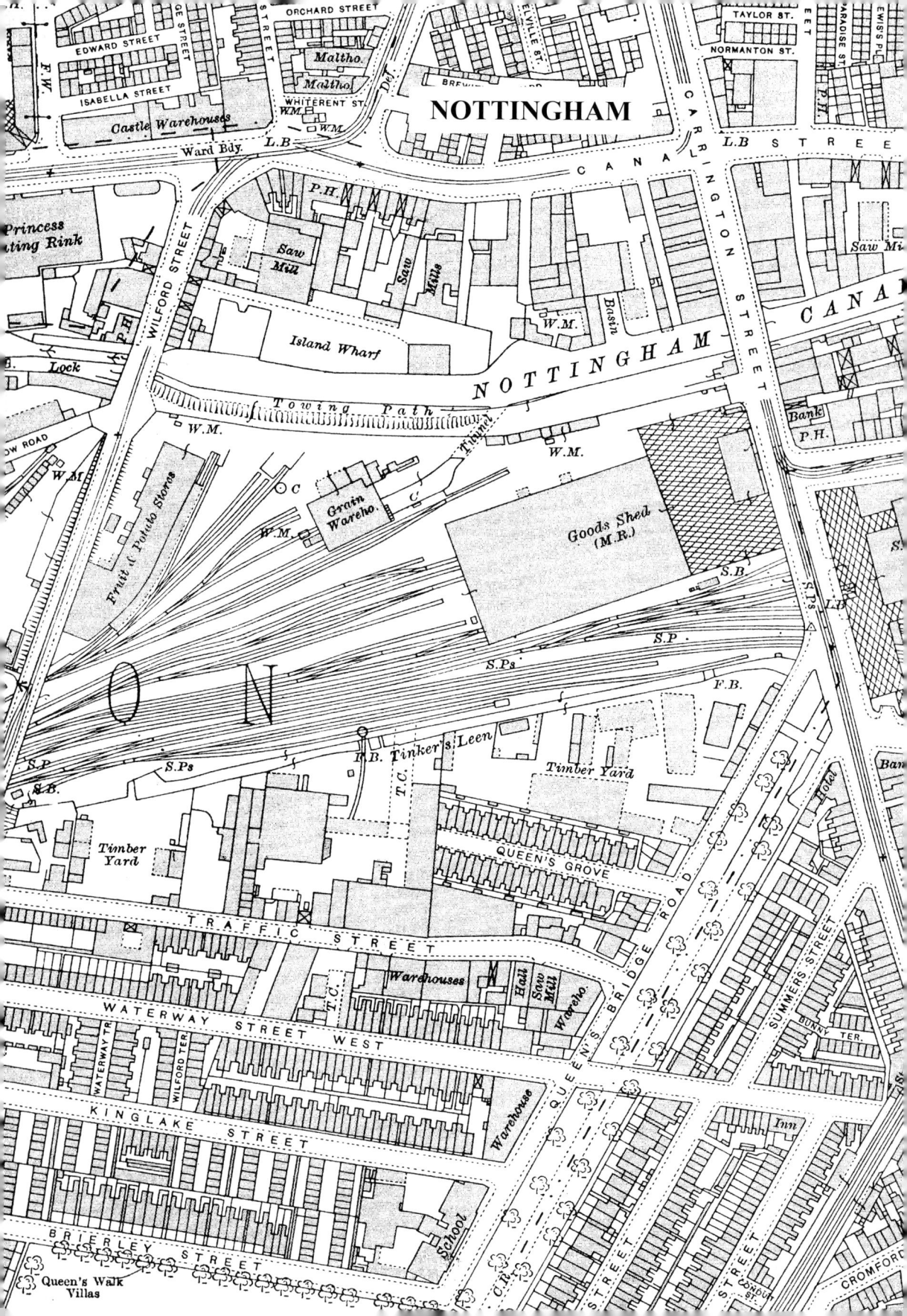

NOTTINGHAM

EDWARD STREET

ORCHARD STREET

TAYLOR ST.

NORMANTON ST.

ISABELLA STREET

Castle Warehouses

Maltho.

Maltho.

WHITERENT ST.

W.M.

W.M.

Ward Bdy.

L.B.

CARRINGTON STREET

L.B STREET

CANAL

Princess ...ting Rink

P.H.

WILFORD STREET

P.H.

Saw Mill

Saw Mills

W.M.

Basin

Saw Mi...

CANAL

Lock

Island Wharf

NOTTINGHAM

Bank

P.H.

...w Road

W.M.

W.M.

Towing Path

Canal

W.M.

Bank

P.H.

W.M.

C

Fruit & Potato Stores

Grain Wareho.

C

Goods Shed (M.R.)

S.B.

S.Ps

W.M.

O N

S.P.

S.Ps

F.B.

S.P.
S.B.

S.Ps

F.B. Tinker's Leen

T.C.

Timber Yard

Timber Yard

QUEEN'S GROVE

BRIDGE ROAD

Hotel

Ban...

TRAFFIC STREET

T.C.

Warehouses

Hall

Saw Mill

Wareho.

SUMMERS STREET

WATERWAY

STREET

WEST

WATERWAY TR.

WILFORD TER.

T.C.

QUEEN'S

BUNNY TER.

KINGLAKE STREET

Warehouses

Inn

BRIERLEY STREET

School

STREET

C.R.

CONDUIT ST.

CROMFOR...

Queen's Walk Villas

MEADOW ST.

Phœnix
Saw Mills

Irongate Wharf

Grain Warehouses

P.H.

S.P.

S.P.

S.P.

Def. TRENT STREET CR.

Factory

Stores

M.P.

School

II.   London Road and its tramway is also on the left border
of the next map. The MR is across this 1915 map and the GCR
vertically, with its Arkwright Street station on the left page,
lower. The engine shed was beyond the left border and was
coded 16A in 1948-63 and 16D until 1965, when it closed.

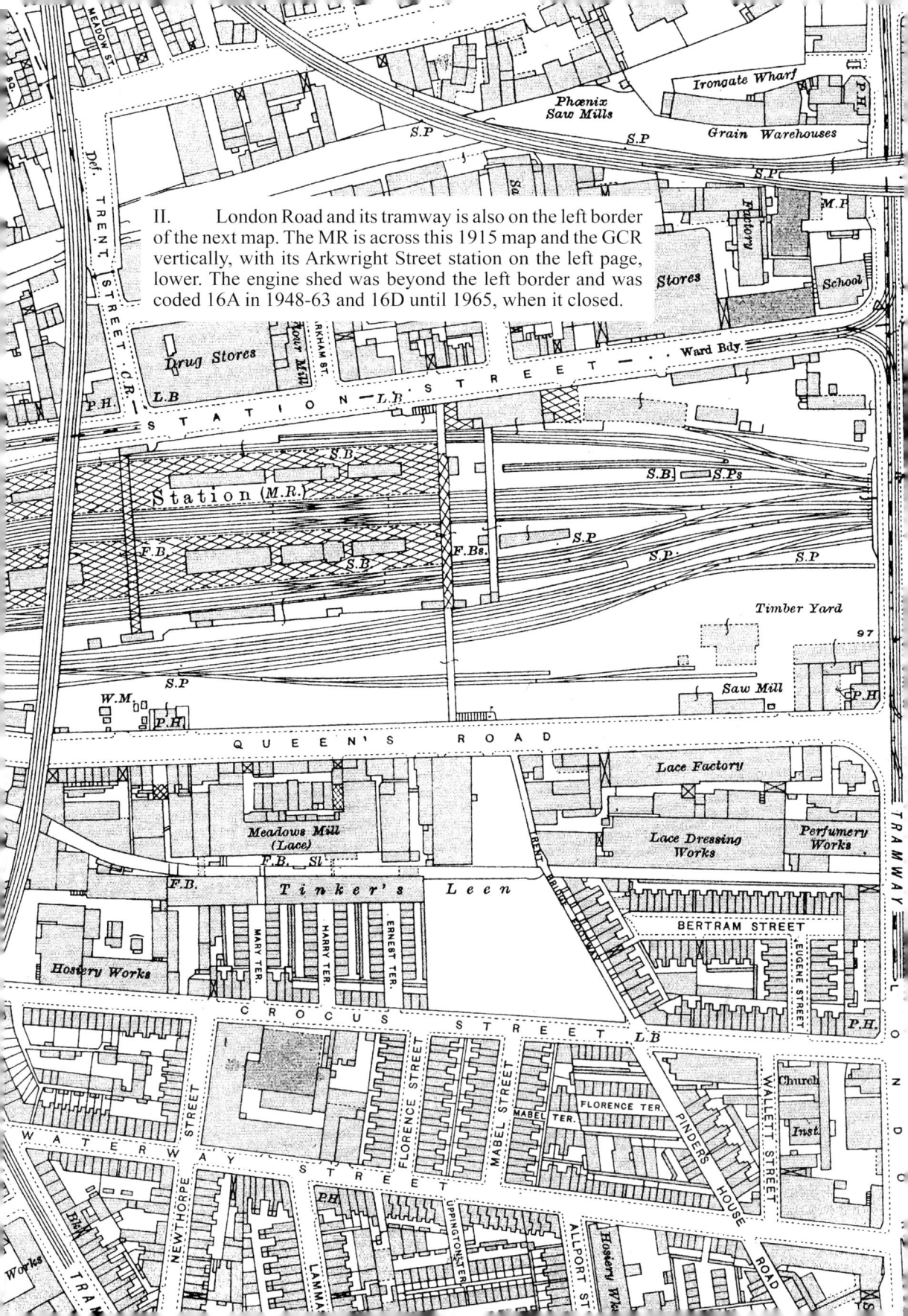

Drug Stores

ARKHAM ST.

COURT MILL

Ward Bdy.

STATION — L.B.

STATION — L.B.

S.B.

S.B.

S.B.

S.Ps

Station (M.R.)

F.B.

F.Bs.

S.P.

S.P.

S.P.

Timber Yard

97

Saw Mill

P.H.

S.P.

W.M.

P.H.

QUEEN'S   ROAD

Lace Factory

Meadows Mill
(Lace)

Lace Dressing
Works

Perfumery
Works

F.B. Sl.

F.B.

Tinker's   Leen

TRENT

BRIDGE RD.

BERTRAM STREET

Hostery Works

MARY TER.

HARRY TER.

ERNEST TER.

EUGENE STREET

P.H.

CROCUS   STREET

L.B

FLORENCE STREET

MABEL STREET

FLORENCE TER.

MABEL TER.

PINDER'S HOUSE

WALLETT STREET

Church

Inst.

WATERWAY

NEWTHORPE STREET

LAMMA

P.H.

UPPINGTON ST.

ALLPORT ST.

Hostery Wks.

TRAMWAY

Works

TRAMWAY   LONDON

1.　　The first station here was a two-tracked terminus with two central sidings. The lines to Lincoln were laid beside it, three years after it opened and trains on the new route had to run into and then reverse out of the station. A new through one was opened on 22nd May 1848, with a long frontage on Station Street. This station was replaced by the one seen on 17th January 1904; it faces Carrington Street and is still in use. Part of Nottingham Corporation Tramways is pictured in 1930. The system was in use from 1901 to 1936. (NRM)

NOTTINGHAM.

A telegraph station.

HOTELS.—George IV., Lion, Flying Horse, Black Boy, Maypole.

MARKET DAYS.—Wednesday and Saturday.

FAIRS.—March 7th and 8th, October 2nd, 3rd, and 4th, Thursday before Easter, and Friday after June 13th.　RACES in July.

BANKERS.—Messrs. J. and J. C. Wright and Co.; Messrs. Smith and Co.; Messrs. Robinson and Moore; Messrs. Hart, Fellowes, and Co.

NOTTINGHAM, the Saxon *Snatinghaham*, and capital of the county of Notts, near the beautiful river Trent, well known to the angler, is situated on a rocky eminence of red sandstone, and is allowed by competent judges to be not only one of the healthiest, but one of the most picturesque inland towns in England.

Extract from Bradshaw's Guide for 1866.
(Reprinted by Middleton Press 2011).
For more details, see page 379 therein.

2.   The final station was recorded, soon after completion. By 2006, there were five through platforms and one bay at the east end. The centre through line was still available. (Lens of Sutton coll.)

3.   A view from 1947 includes class 2F 0-6-0 LMS no. 3458, a type dating back to the MR in 1878. The bridge above it was built for the 1897 main line of the GCR. (H.C.Casserley)

4. Gently hissing on 14th July 1947 is class 4F 0-6-0 no. 4004, ex-MR. The station suffix was "City" from 25th September 1950 and "Midland" from 18th June 1951 until 6th May 1970. Demolition of the GCR bridge across the platforms took place in 1980, the last freight using it in 1968. (H.C.Casserley)

5. An eastward view in about 1948 includes an LMS 4-4-0 and extremely complex signal brackets. An amazing 48 private sidings had been recorded in 1904. (Milepost 92½)

6. A trolleybus is seen on 27th May 1959. Its system was in use from 1927 until 1966. Carrington Street and its bridge over the MR had been widened in 1902. (H.C.Casserley)

For more views of trolleybuses in Nottingham, please see
Nottinghamshire & Derbyshire Trolleybuses **(Middleton Press)**

---

7. This is an eastward view in 1957. In 1950, BR had employed 85 horses here and there was a staff of over 400 five years later. In 1947, the island platforms became real islands, when the Trent flooded the tracks. (Stations UK)

8.   Ex-LMS class 4P no. 40936 presented a fine sight at the head of the RCTS 'Lincolnshire Rail Tour' on 16th May 1954. This type had three cylinders and was produced from 1924. (H.Ballantyne)

9.   Platforms 4 and 5 were designed for 18 coaches, 1 and 3 for 20, 6 for 14 and bay 2 for five. At 4a on 6th July 1975 is the 16.22 Lincoln to Crewe and at no. 3 is the 17.05 Derby to Lincoln. (T.Heavyside)

10.   Trams returned to terminate outside the station on 9th March 2004. Work began in 2013 to extend the route south, this necessitating the construction of a new bridge on the site of the GCR one over the platforms. The station roof and the new abutment can be seen in the foreground of this photograph from 15th February 2013. (D.Hanger)

Full details of the system are in Section 4 of
***Triumphant Tramways* (Middleton Press 2009).**

ISLAND STREET

Factory

Drug Factory

Warehouse

C

F.B.

G. N.

W.M.

EAST OF NOTTINGHAM

1304a
3·755

S.B.

W.M.

Chy.

London Road
Station
(High Level)

Goods Shed
(G.N.R.)

W.M.

Goods Shed
(G.N.R.)

Goods She
(G.N.R.)

97

S.Ps.

London Road Station
(Low Level)
(G.N.R.)

S.B.

London Road Junction

S.B.

S.P.

S.Ps.

Carriage Shed

S.Ps.

S.Ps.

T.C.

S.Ps.

Timber Yard

S.Ps.

Tank

Saw Mill

S.Ps.

S.P.

W.M.

W.Ms.

TRAMWAY

Tank

L
O
N
D
O
N

86

Refuse
Destructor

Chy.

Refuse
Destructor

Cattle Pens

East Croft
(Corporation Depôt)

BASIN

DRY
DOCK

Banks

STREET

Cattle
Pens

T.C.

S.P

S.B

SNEINTON HERMITAGE

SNEINTON HERMITAGE TRAMWAY

THORESBY AVENUE

S.P

L. & N.W.R.

GOODS BRANCH

S.P

LINDU

W.M.

Cattle Pens

S.P

S.P

S.Ps

S.P

S.P

S.P

S.B.

S.P.

S.B.

S.P

F.B.

S.B.

S.B.

S.Ps

S.Ps

Sneinton Junction

W.M.

M.P

S.P

P.O.

Mission
Church

W

L

A

N

E

GRAING

HOLME STREET

MEA

STREET

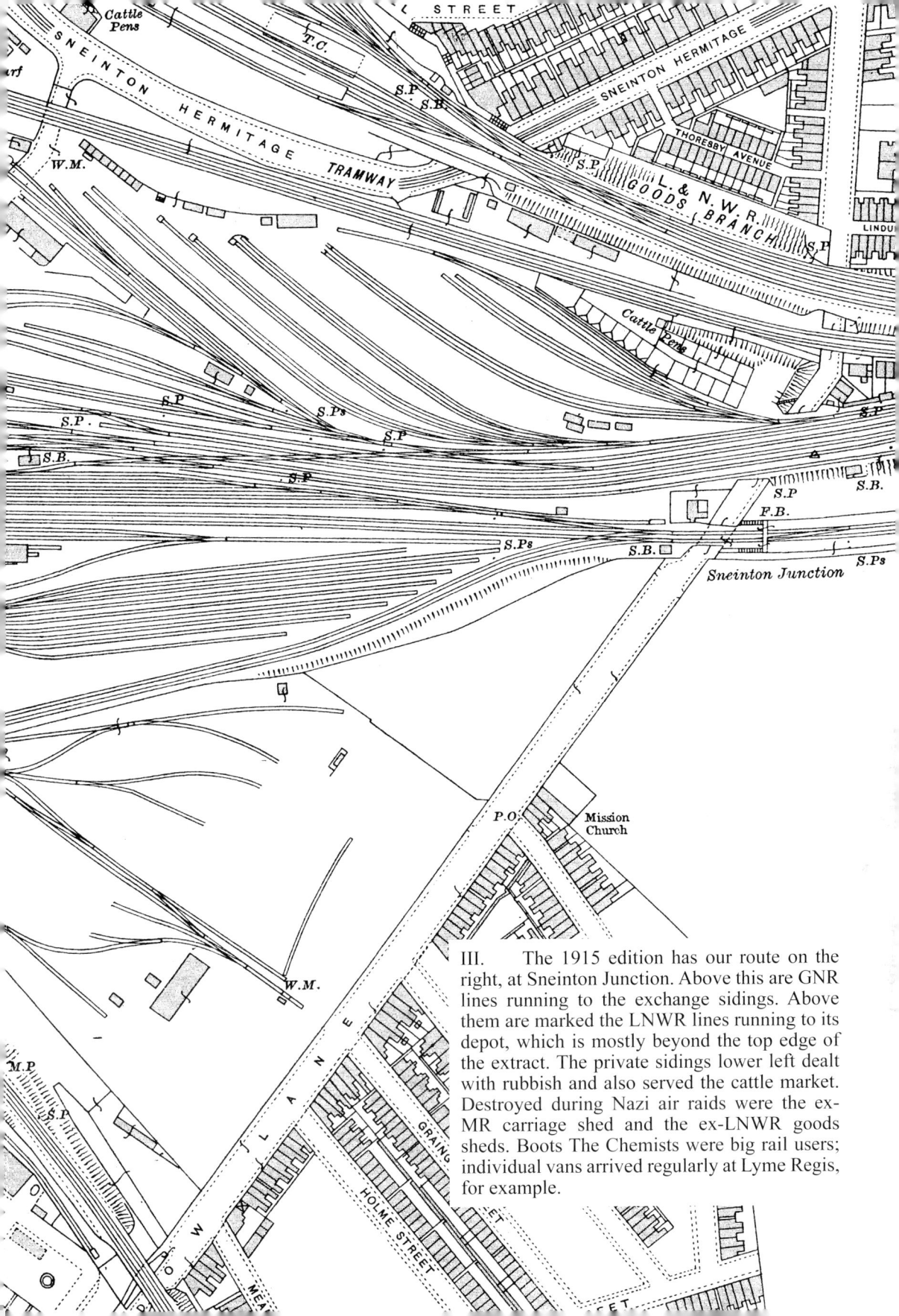

III.   The 1915 edition has our route on the
right, at Sneinton Junction. Above this are GNR
lines running to the exchange sidings. Above
them are marked the LNWR lines running to its
depot, which is mostly beyond the top edge of
the extract. The private sidings lower left dealt
with rubbish and also served the cattle market.
Destroyed during Nazi air raids were the ex-
MR carriage shed and the ex-LNWR goods
sheds. Boots The Chemists were big rail users;
individual vans arrived regularly at Lyme Regis,
for example.

↑ 11.   This panorama is from the footbridge on the right of map III and Nottingham station is just beyond London Road bridge, in the distance. Seen on 3rd May 1993 is BR 2-6-4T no. 80080, working "The Jolly Fisherman" special to Skegness. On the right is the ex-GNR signal box. (T.Heavyside)

← 12.   A different lens used from the same bridge on 27th July 1984 includes Sneinton Junction box. Its 30-lever frame was still in use in 2013. A Swindon-built DMU is working the 09.07 Birmingham New Street to Lincoln St. Marks service. The city's castle is situated on the high ground on the right. (P.D.Shannon)

13.   A view in the opposite direction from London Road bridge on 30th June 2006 shows that a new road bridge has replaced the footbridge used for the two previous photographs. No. 66126 is hauling empty coal wagons from Immingham to Margam. To the right of the train is the Nottingham Light Maintenance Depot and to the right of that is Eastcroft Depot of the track engineers. (P.D.Shannon)

14.   London Road Junction is seen from London Road, looking east with the route to Kettering curving right. It carried passengers from 1879 and was operated by the MR. Closure came in 1968. The box had 80 levers and closed on 7th December 1969. Most goods facilities were withdrawn in 1967. The location is now known as Nottingham East Junction. (Milepost 92½)

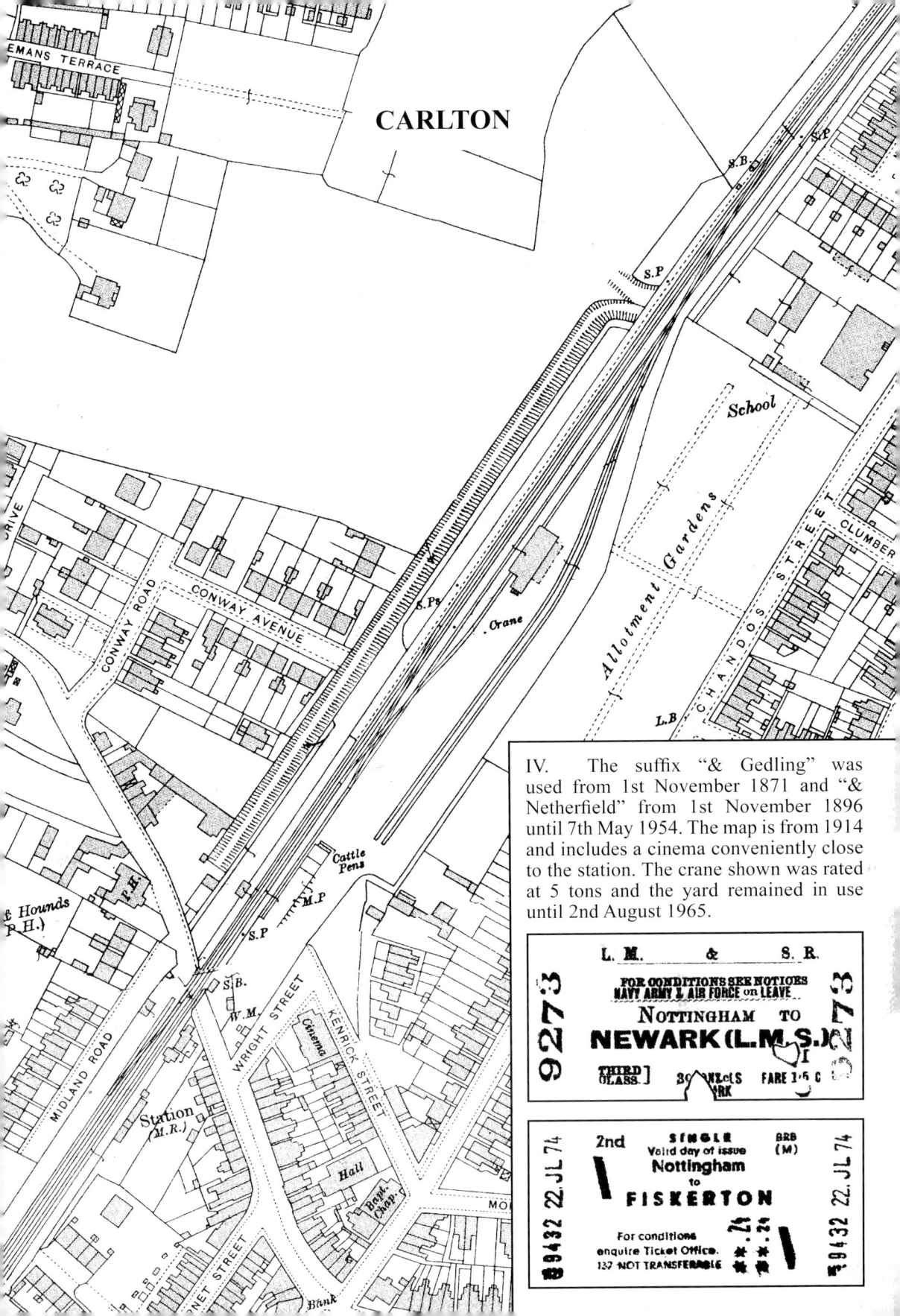

CARLTON

IV. The suffix "& Gedling" was used from 1st November 1871 and "& Netherfield" from 1st November 1896 until 7th May 1954. The map is from 1914 and includes a cinema conveniently close to the station. The crane shown was rated at 5 tons and the yard remained in use until 2nd August 1965.

9273

L. M. & S. R.
FOR CONDITIONS SEE NOTICES
NAVY ARMY & AIR FORCE on LEAVE
NOTTINGHAM TO
NEWARK (L.M.S.)
THIRD CLASS] 3d NIGHTS PARK FARE 1·6 C

9432 22 JL 74
2nd SINGLE BRB (M)
Valid day of issue
Nottingham
to
FISKERTON
For conditions enquire Ticket Office.
137 NOT TRANSFERABLE

Labels on map: LEMANS TERRACE, S.B., S.P., School, Allotment Gardens, CHANDOS STREET, CLUMBER, DRIVE, Crane, CONWAY ROAD, CONWAY AVENUE, L.B., Cattle Pens, & Hounds (P.H.), P.H., M.P., S.P., S.B., W.M., Midland Road, WRIGHT STREET, KENRICK STREET, Cinema, Station (M.R.), Hall, Bapt. Chap., NET STREET, Bank, MO...

15.　　The station is behind the horse and trap; in front of the crossing lamp is a lady with a long skirt and an appropriate chain guard on her bicycle. (P.Laming coll.)

16.　　A view in the other direction includes extensive granite setts, the pedestrian wicket gate and a telegraph pole, with offset insulator bars. Enjoy this variety in picture 15 and consider explanations. (P.Laming coll.)

17.   A July 1961 panorama includes the 20-lever signal box and its gate wheel. They were taken out of use on 28th September 1980. Near Nottingham, the route runs at the foot of the sandstone cliffs, which are on the north side of the line. (H.C.Casserley)

18.   The chained up foot crossing is seen on 22nd July 1961. The arrangement was altered before the station ceased to be staffed on 2nd November 1969. (H.C.Casserley)

19.   The young spotter watches the 12.45 Lincoln to Coventry call on 21st September 1991. Both the staggered platforms have brick built shelters. The platform lengths are for six coaches on the down side and five on the up. (A.C.Hartless)

BURTON JOYCE

ST. HELEN'S GROVE

Station

Cattle Pen

NOTTINGHA

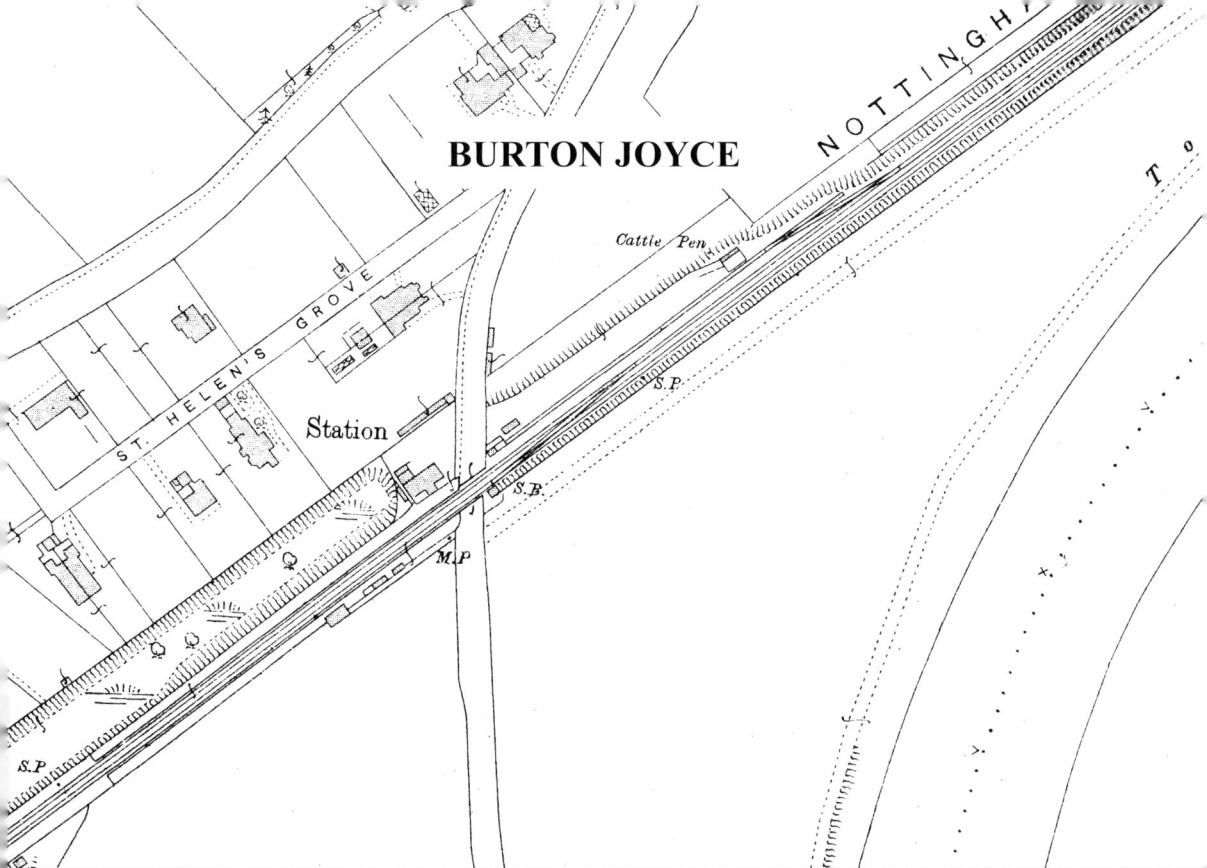

V. Large dwellings began to appear not long before the 1914 edition was produced, but one siding was sufficient.

20. A train arrives from Lincoln as everyone faces the postcard photographer and we enjoy the tidiness. The building on the right appears to be younger than the others; probably a flat-pack one. (P.Laming coll.)

21. The map shows a crossover, but it had gone by the time of this postcard, probably the 1920s. Note the slope up to the platform and the busy siding. (Lens of Sutton coll.)

22. The signal box had 18 levers and served as a ground frame from 11th October 1970. It is seen on 1st September 1956, as a train arrives from the Newark direction. (Milepost 92½)

23.   Many of the stations had shelters designed to withstand heavy snowfall. This one is seen with its fire buckets, as a DMU approaches on 13th July 1963. (B.W.L.Brooksbank)

24.   A young observer watches nos 31255 and 31154 pass through the featureless station on 21st September 1991, hauling empty fuel tanks to Killingholme. The down platform takes six coaches and the up one five. (A.C.Hartless)

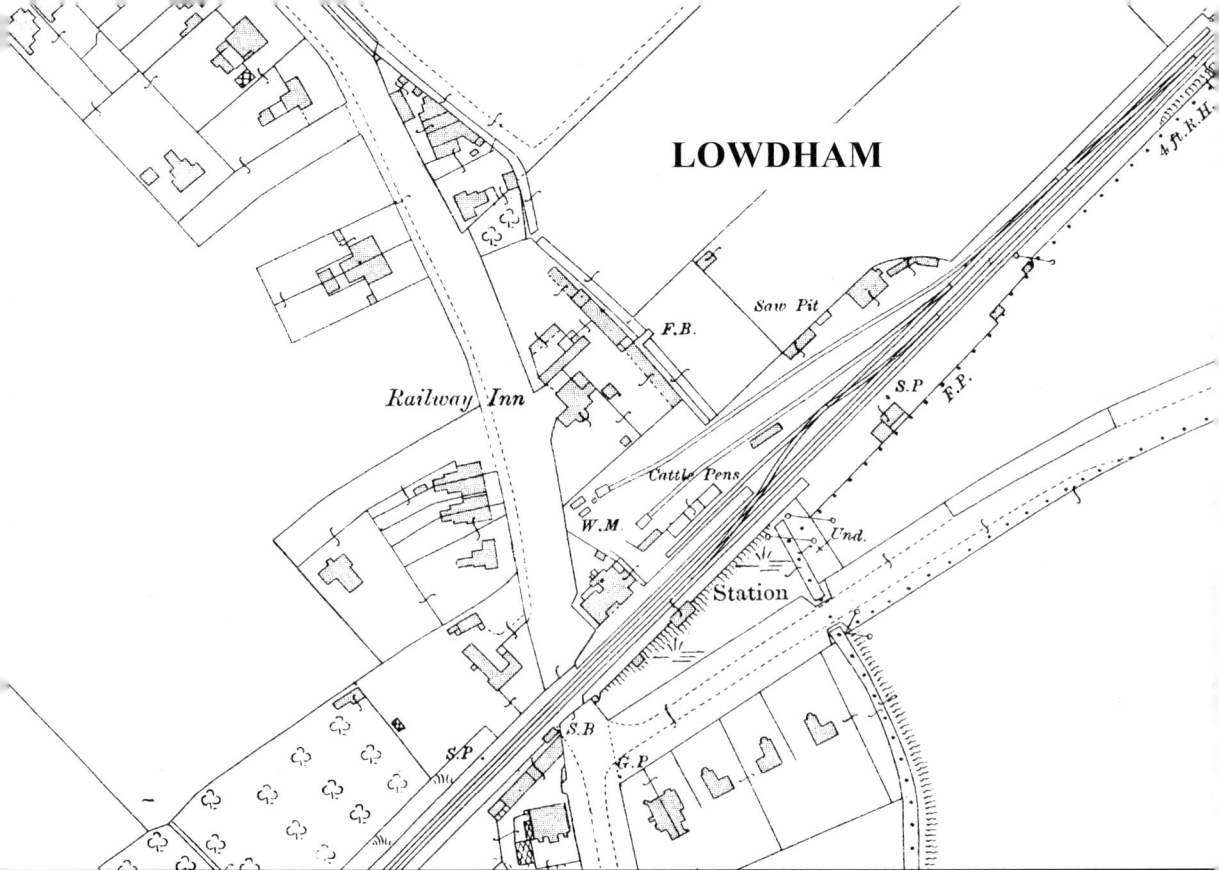

LOWDHAM

Railway Inn

Saw Pit

F.B.

Cattle Pens

S.P. F.P.

W.M.

Und.

Station

S.P.

S.B.

G.P.

VI.   The 1914 map is scaled at 20ins to 1 mile and includes an inn, missing at most locations on the route.

25.   Assorted chimney pots are of note on this card, which was posted in September 1908 to the Railway Inn at Thorpe-on-the-Hill. (P.Laming coll.)

26.   Another postcard and this confirms the presence of four gates here. Some of the complex operating mechanism is evident. (P.Laming coll.)

27.   The oil lighting of the previous picture has given way to electric and the end of steam is nigh; the number on the platform is for the benefit of DMU drivers. Class 3P 2-6-2T no. 42330 is arriving from Nottingham on 28th August 1959. (Milepost 92½)

28.   A view from the signal box on the same day includes the goods yard and a non-railway crane, known as shear legs. It was used for timber. Freight traffic ceased on 16th June 1964. (Milepost 92½)

29.   A Leicester to Grimsby Town service arrives on 25th July 2005, worked by no. 158780. Although the platform could still take six coaches, a 3-car train had to come to this end of it. (P.D.Shannon)

30.   Seen on the same day is no. 156410 working the 15.35 Lincoln to Leicester. The engineers siding is rather overgrown. Goods had been its earlier use. The platform on the left was fit for 4-car trains. (P.D.Shannon)

L M. & S. R.
FOR CONDITIONS SEE NOTICES
Carlton & Netherf'ld to
LOWDHAM
9930   9930
THIRD
CLASS]   365 (S)   FARE -/8½ C

MIDLAND   RAILWAY.   This Ticket is
issued subject to the Regulations & Conditions
stated in the Company's Time Tables & Bills.
THIRD CLASS.   THIRD CLASS.
AVAILABLE ON DAY OF ISSUE ONLY.
CARLTON & NETHERFIELD to
THURGARTON
21 MAY 38   1501   1501
FARE 6½d.   FARE 6½d.
Carlton&N Thurgart.   Alton&N Thurgarton

THURGARTON

(map annotations: S.P., NOTTINGHA, W.M., Thurgarton Station, P, S.B., 80)

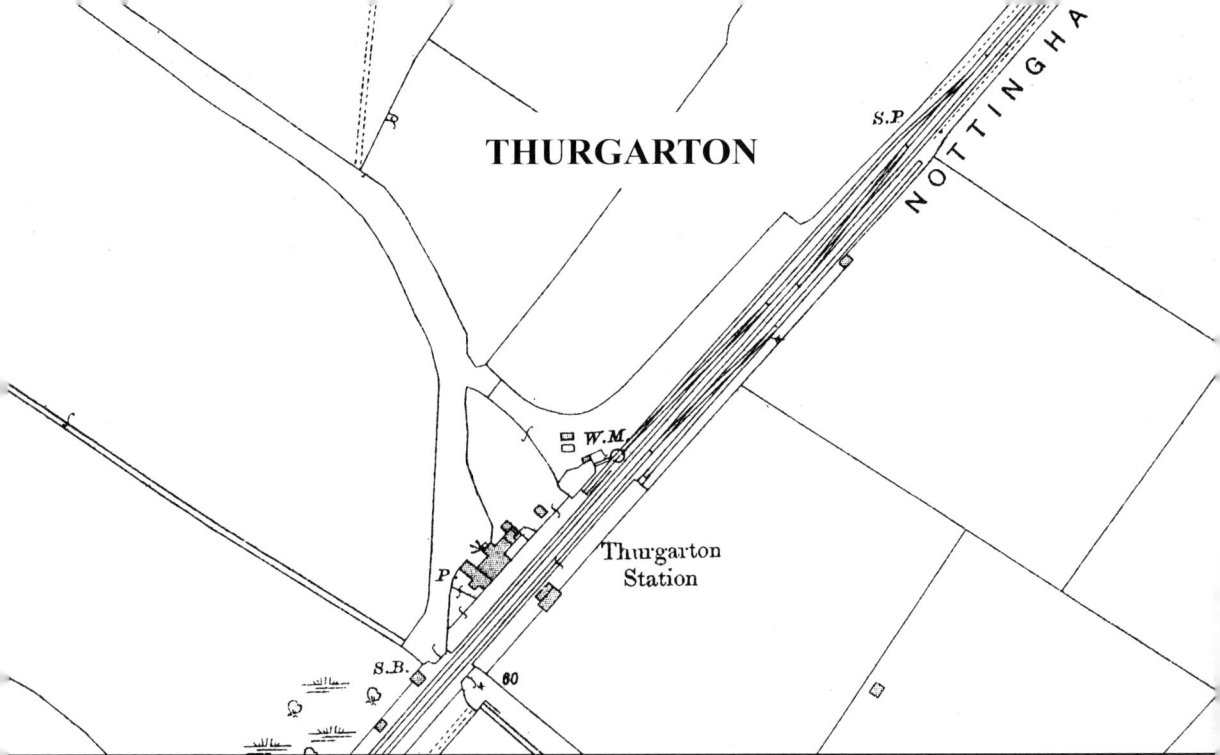

VII. There were no dwellings near the station in 1920, but there were some sidings.

31.   An early overview is provided by two well composed postcards. No ankles were to be seen, in those days. (P.Laming coll.)

32.   The single gate system was applied here again. The signal box was completed in 1902 and had a 16-lever frame. (Lens of Sutton coll.)

1244	2nd-SINGLE SINGLE-2nd	1244
	Lowdham to	
	Lowdham Lowdham	
	Newark (Castle) Newark (Castle)	
	NEWARK (CASTLE)	
	(E) 2/6 Fare 2/6 (E)	
	For conditions see over For conditions see over	

4809	3rd- SINGLE SINGLE -3rd	4809
	Lowdham to	
	Lowdham Lowdham	
	Thurgarton Thurgarton	
	THURGARTON	
	(E) 6d. FARE 6d. (E)	
	For conditions see over For conditions see over	

2735	2nd-SINGLE SINGLE-2nd	2735
	Thurgarton to	
	Thurgarton Thurgarton	
	Bleasby Bleasby	
	BLEASBY	
	(E) 0/6 Fare 0/6 (E)	
	For conditions see over For conditions see over	

443	L. M. & S. R.
	Issued subject to the conditions & regulations in the Cos Time Tables Books Bills & Notices and in the Railway Cos Book of regulations relating to traffic by Passenger train or other similar service
	Thurgarton to
	LOWDHAM
	THIRD CLASS] 3653 (S) Fare -/3½ Lowdham

33. The picture is from 11th May 1957. The box was reduced to the status of a ground frame on 4th October 1970 and was closed on 8th March 1982. The goods yard closed on 7th December 1964. (Milepost 92½)

34. Again staggered platforms were created, a boon to impatient motorists. They are seen in March 2013, both platforms are of four-car length. (K.Knott)

BLEASBY

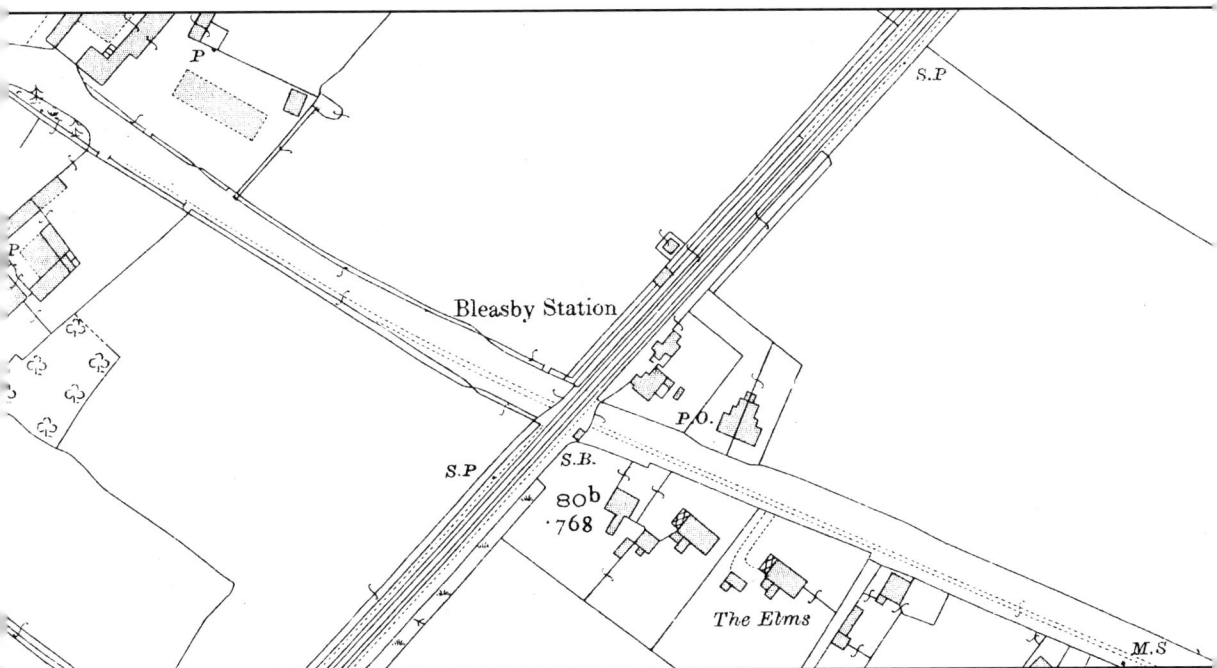

VIII.   Another 1919 extract and this reveals a little more habitation than elsewhere on this route. The suffix "Gate" was applied until 1889.

35.   The station opened in December 1848 and initially demand was so low that trains called on Wednesdays only. Saturdays were added from November 1849. (Lens of Sutton coll.)

36.   A daily service did not start until July 1863, but a goods service was never offered. Granite setts were provided on the crossings, as was the case on most street tramways, in their early years. (Lens of Sutton coll.)

37.   The level crossing had a five-lever ground frame until 16th December 1973, when automatic half barriers came into use. By that time, the platforms were staggered. This and the next picture date from 25th July 2005. (P.D.Shannon)

38. No. 170114 has the destination Nottingham, while plants with wind seed dispersal systems expand their colonies, thanks to the draught from trains. The platforms take four cars each. The up one is accessed by a long path, which is hidden by the train. (P.D.Shannon)

MIDLAND RAILWAY.
This Ticket is issued subject to the Regulations &
Conditions stated in the Co.'s Time Tables & Bills.
THIRD CLASS.   THIRD CLASS.
AVAILABLE ON DAY OF ISSUE ONLY.
Thurgarton   to
NOTTINGHAM
REVISED FARE 1/5½   REVISED FARE 1/5½
Thurgarton-Nott'm   Thurgarton-Nott'm

BRITISH RLYS. (E)   BRITISH RLYS. (E)
For conditions   For conditions
see back   see back
Available for three days   Available for three days
including day of issue   including day of issue
Bleasby   Bleasby
" BLEASBY to
ROLLESTON JUNC.
ROLLESTON JCT.   ROLLESTON JCT.
3rd.   6d.Z   3rd.   6d.Z

FISKERTON

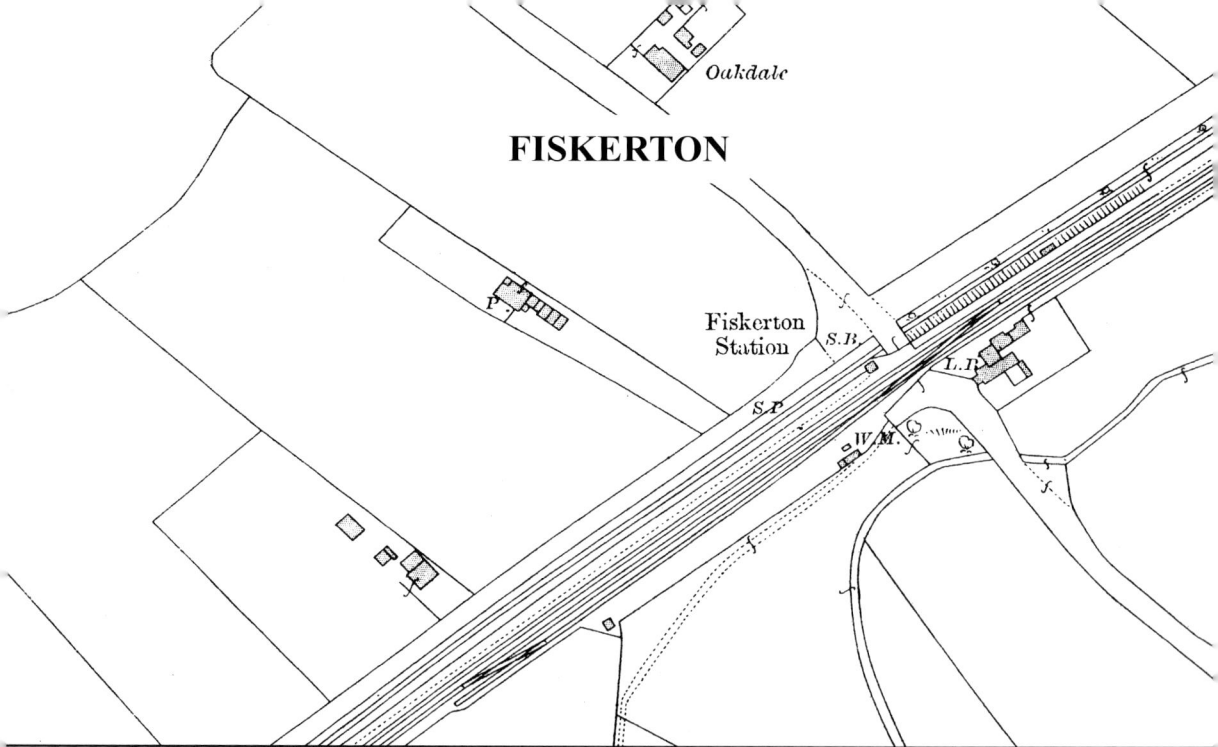

IX. A 1919 extract includes a goods loop, which was in use until 15th June 1964.

39.   The elaborate building was photographed in 1948, when track inspection was in progress. A wicket gate was provided for pedestrians for generations. The parcels shed appears to be full. (Stations UK)

40.   The box was built in about 1902 and had 16-levers after being demoted to a gate box in 1934. It is seen on 23rd June 1999, as no. 153333 departs for Nottingham. Five coach trains can stand at either platform. (A.C.Hartless)

41.   Pictured on the same day, the box had no gate wheel and so the staff were kept fit. The small gate was for their use only. (A.C.Hartless)

42.   Half a mile to the west, Fiskerton Junction box was also still in use in 2013. The junction had not existed since 1965; it is shown on map I. It contains a gate wheel and 30 levers. The connection to Southwell had been double track, but seldom carried passengers. (B.Bennett)

ROLLESTON JUNCTION

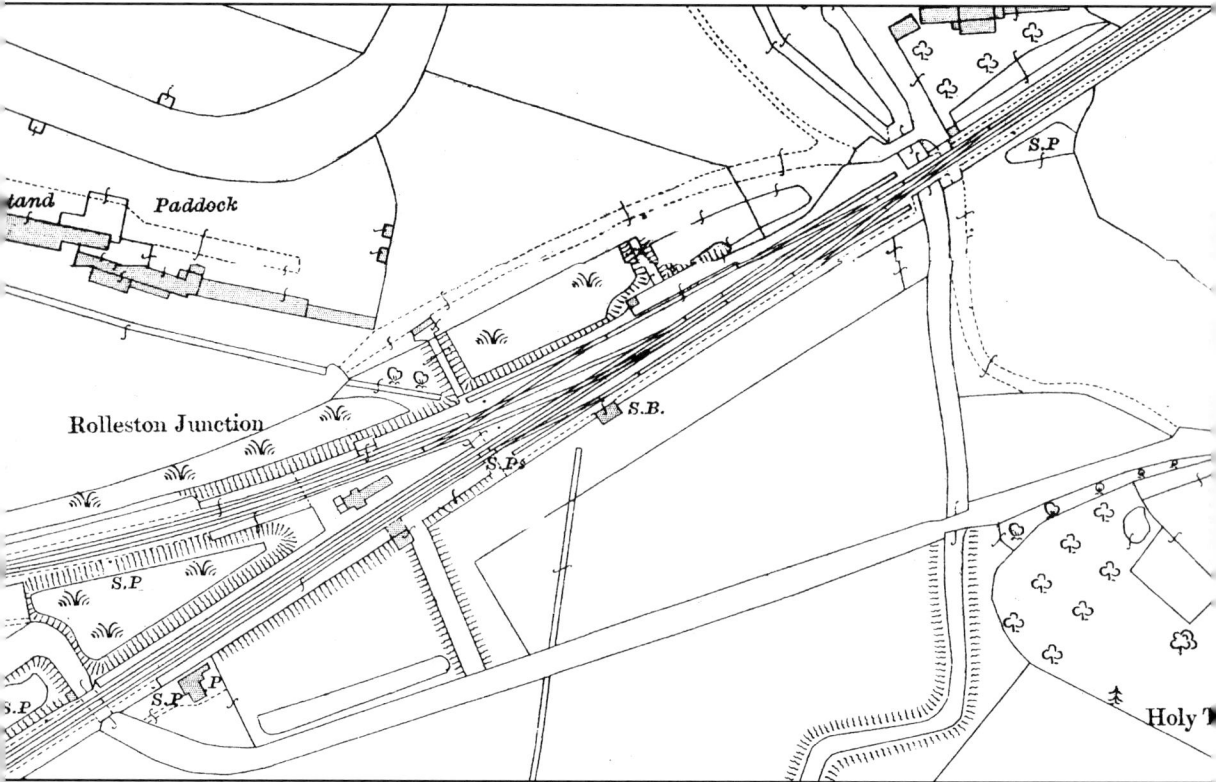

X. The 1919 edition has our route diagonally and the Southwell branch curving from it.

43. A train from Nottingham approaches as we enjoy the unusual styling of the design of the station. It opened as Southwell Junction on 1st July 1847 and closed on 1st August 1849. It reopened on 12th April 1852 and closed again on 14th March 1853. It was revived as Rolleston on 1st September 1860, the suffix "Junction" being added in November of that year. (P.Laming coll.)

44.   This is the Southwell branch train at 7.38pm on 30th August 1947, propelled by 0-4-4T no. 1324. In the background is 2-6-4T no. 2328 with the connecting service, known as the "Tamworth Mail". (W.A.Camwell/SLS coll.)

45.   A 1948 panorama features the foot crossing which was in universal use. There was no goods traffic at this station. The building was erected in 1871 and the line northwards was doubled in 1921. (Stations UK)

46.   The "Southwell Paddy" was worked by ex-MR 0-4-4T no. 58085 on 9th June 1956. The class 1P was introduced in 1881. (H.C.Casserley)

47.	The Southwell "Motor Train" was hauled by no. 58065 on 31st May 1958 and it is about to depart for Newark. This was its last full year of operation and the buildings would soon be demolished. The term "Junction" was dropped on 7th May 1973. (R.S.Carpenter)

ROLLESTON

48.   Behind the photographer is a road crossing and on the gates is a sign stating "Please use crossing bell provided to obtain attendant. Do not use car horn". No. 66200 is hauling coal from Immingham to Ketton on 25th July 2005. Both platforms can hold seven coaches. (P.D.Shannon)

WEST OF NEWARK

49.   Just under three miles from Newark Castle station is Staythorpe Crossing. Power station 'A' was opened nearby in 1950 and increasing coal traffic meant that the frame had to be enlarged from 20 to 35 levers in the 1960s. Staythorpe 'B' opened in 1962. 'A' was demolished in 1989 and 'B' followed in 1995. The boundary of the Eastern Region was nearby from 1986. The class 120 DMU is working the 18.45 Lincoln St. Marks to Crewe on 26th July 1984 and is near the coal siding points. The box was still in use in 2013. (P.D.Shannon)

NEWARK CASTLE

Football Ground

XI. The 1920 edition has the River Trent lower right, with the Great North Road crossing it and the GNR. The road was numbered A1 from 1919 until 1964. The nearby works was noted for wheelwrighting, agricultural implements and for creating a sugar beet lifter in the late 1920s. The Newark Curve is the centre one of the three, top right. Lower centre is the 1886 cattle market, which demanded over 1000 wagon movements annually for over 40 years. The suffix "Castle" was added on 29th May 1950. North Box is near the top of the map; its 20-lever frame was in use until 21st March 1965. It had been damaged in a shunting accident on 21st April 1964.

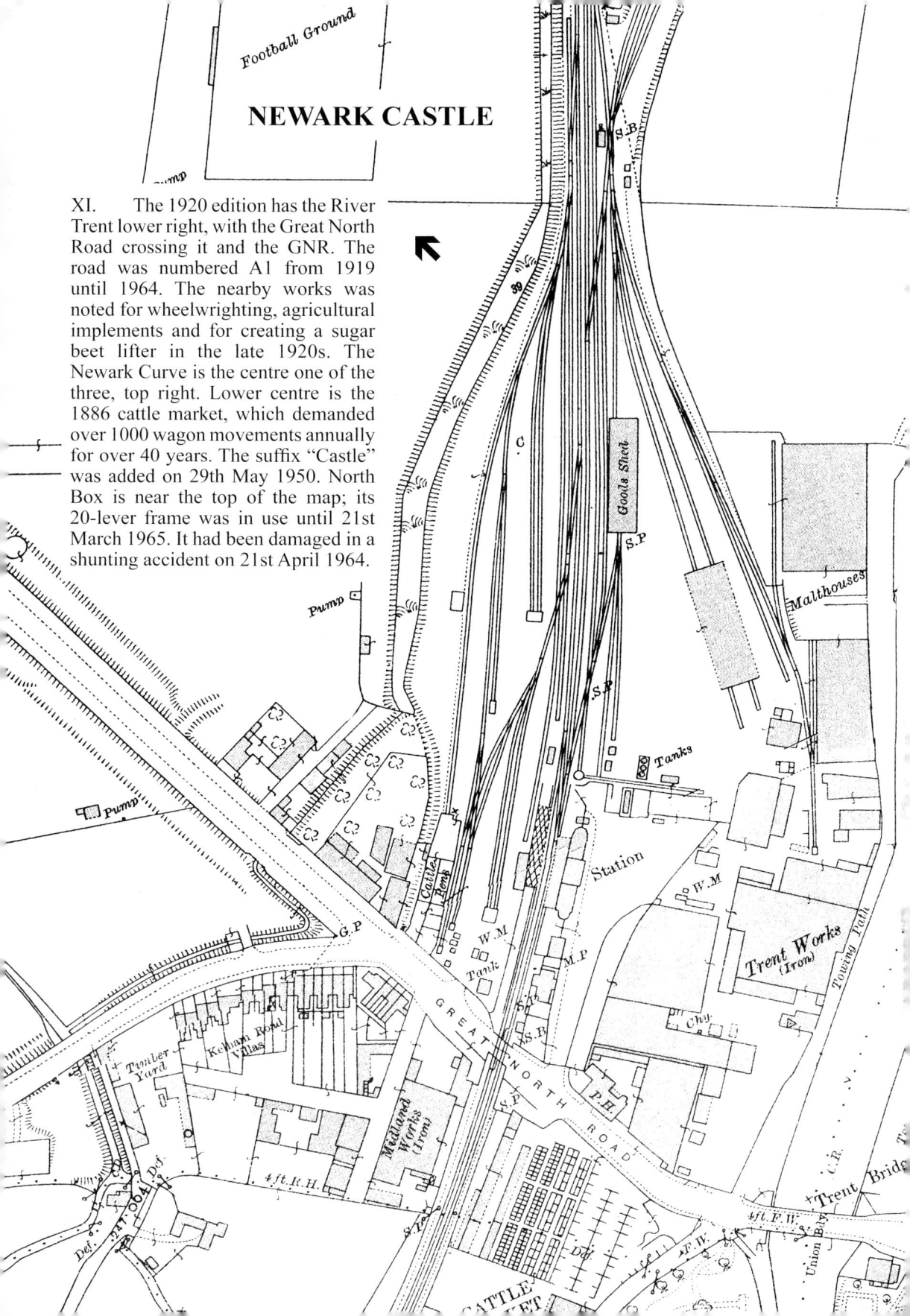

S.B.

Pump

Pump

Goods Shed

S.P.

S.P.

S.P.

Malthouses

Tanks

Pump

C

Station

W.M.

G.P.

Castle Bank

W.M.

Tank

M.P.

Trent Works (Iron)

Towing Path

Timber Yard

Kelham Road Villas

Midland Works (Iron)

Chy.

P.H.

S.B.

S.P.

GREAT NORTH ROAD

Def.

4ft. R.H.

CATTLE MARKET

Union Bdy.

Trent Bridge

4ft. F.W.

4ft. F.W.

C.R.

50.   The MR created these premises at the time of the line opening, the main buildings being on the town side. There was a population of about 10,000 in 1841, this increasing to 15,000 by 1901 and 24,000 by 1961. (P.Laming coll.)

51.   Calling with a train bound for Nottingham sometime in the 1950s is 2-6-2T no. 40168. The LMS introduced this class 3P in 1935. The original up platform canopy lasted until 1953 and its replacement was removed in 1995. (W.A.Camwell/SLS coll.)

52.　　The goods shed was completed in 1871 and is seen in the 1960s, by which time the down platform had lost its weather protection. The goods yard closed on 4th April 1983; there had been a coal depot at Cross Street until 1st November 1971. It was accessed from the Newark Curve. The brickwork on the left has not survived. (Lens of Sutton coll.)

Extract from Bradshaw's Guide for 1866.
(Reprinted by Middleton Press 2011).
For more details, see page 426 therein.

NEWARK.

A telegraph station.

HOTEL.—Clinton Arms, family and commercial, and posting house.

MARKET DAY.—Wednesday.

FAIRS. — May 14th, Whit Tuesday, Aug. 2nd, Wednesday before Oct. 2nd, Nov. 1st and Monday before Dec. 12th.

The fine parish Church of *St. Mary*, near the Market Place, is a noble cross, rebuilt in the later Gothic style in place of an earlier one, of which the Norman base of the tall spire is a remnant. The apostles stand in niches round the spire, and they are also carved on the shaft of the font. Most of the spouts, &c., end in grotesque heads. The tower is light, and the tracery of the windows elegant and good; several of which are stained. A carved screen fronts the choir, at the end of which is the "Raising of Lazarus" by Hilton. Besides the arms of neighbouring families there is a curious brass, under a three-arched canopy in the south transept of Alan Flemynge, the supposed founder of the church; he has curly hair, coat, mantle, sleeves buttoned at the wristbands, and pointed boots; the date, 1361. The interior has been recently restored, under the superintendence of Mr. Scott, and is now one of the finest parish churches in the kingdom.

53.   The signal box is seen on 9th October 1976. Its 16-lever frame was still in use in 2013. The 13.37 Lincoln St. Marks to Crewe is crossing the old A1. The down platform takes four cars and the up one three. (T.Heavyside)

54.   The classic exterior was recorded in August 2008. There were 26 private sidings serving the industrious town in 1904, the figure rising to 34 by 1938. The output included malt, various engineering products, sugar (from 1921) and gypsum. (Milepost 92½)

XII. The MR map of about 1920 shows the connection between the GNR and the MR which was known as the Newark Curve. It was open from 1869 until 1973, but it did not carry a regular passenger service. It has enabled DMUs on our route to run in and out of Newark North Gate regularly.

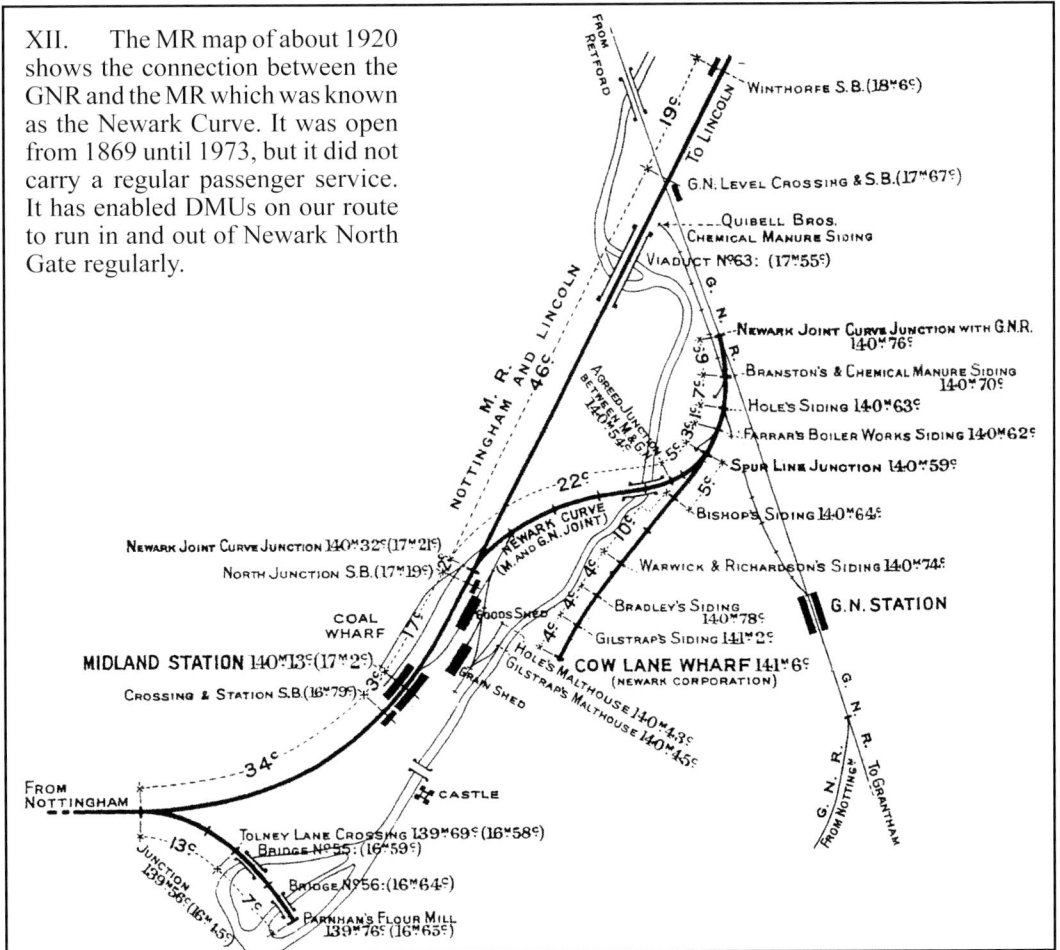

WINTHORPE S.B. (18ᴹ6ᶜ)

G.N. LEVEL CROSSING & S.B. (17ᴹ67ᶜ)

QUIBELL BROS. CHEMICAL MANURE SIDING

VIADUCT Nº63: (17ᴹ55ᶜ)

NEWARK JOINT CURVE JUNCTION WITH G.N.R. 140ᴹ76ᶜ

BRANSTON'S & CHEMICAL MANURE SIDING 140ᴹ70ᶜ

HOLE'S SIDING 140ᴹ63ᶜ

FARRAR'S BOILER WORKS SIDING 140ᴹ62ᶜ

SPUR LINE JUNCTION 140ᴹ59ᶜ

BISHOP'S SIDING 140ᴹ64ᶜ

WARWICK & RICHARDSON'S SIDING 140ᴹ74ᶜ

G.N. STATION

NEWARK JOINT CURVE JUNCTION 140ᴹ32ᶜ(17ᴹ21ᶜ)

NORTH JUNCTION S.B. (17ᴹ19ᶜ)

AGREED JUNCTION BETWEEN M & G.N. 140ᴹ54ᶜ

NEWARK CURVE (M. AND G.N. JOINT)

BRADLEY'S SIDING 140ᴹ78ᶜ

GILSTRAP'S SIDING 141ᴹ2ᶜ

COAL WHARF

GOODS SHED

GRAIN SHED

MIDLAND STATION 140ᴹ13ᶜ(17ᴹ2ᶜ)

CROSSING & STATION S.B.(16ᴹ79ᶜ)

HOLE'S MALTHOUSE

GILSTRAP'S MALTHOUSE 140ᴹ43ᶜ 140ᴹ45ᶜ

COW LANE WHARF 141ᴹ6ᶜ (NEWARK CORPORATION)

CASTLE

FROM NOTTINGHAM

TOLNEY LANE CROSSING 139ᴹ69ᶜ(16ᴹ58ᶜ)

BRIDGE Nº55: (16ᴹ59ᶜ)

BRIDGE Nº56: (16ᴹ64ᶜ)

PARNHAM'S FLOUR MILL 139ᴹ76ᶜ (16ᴹ65ᶜ)

JUNCTION 139ᴹ56ᶜ(16ᴹ45ᶜ)

FROM RETFORD

TO LINCOLN

NOTTINGHAM M.R. AND LINCOLN 46ᶜ

G.N.R. TO GRANTHAM

G.N.R. FROM NOTTINGHAM

55. The ex-GNR main line is across the picture, while the route to Lincoln runs into the distance. The signal box was known as Newark Crossing and was in use until 17th May 1981. It had 12 levers. A DMU is on the curve soon after it was opened in March 1965. (C.T.Gifford)

56.   We now look north along the main line to Retford and have the 1965 curve on the right. The crossing of the routes is to the left of the signal box, in this 1970 view.
(H.B.Priestley/picturethepast.org.uk)

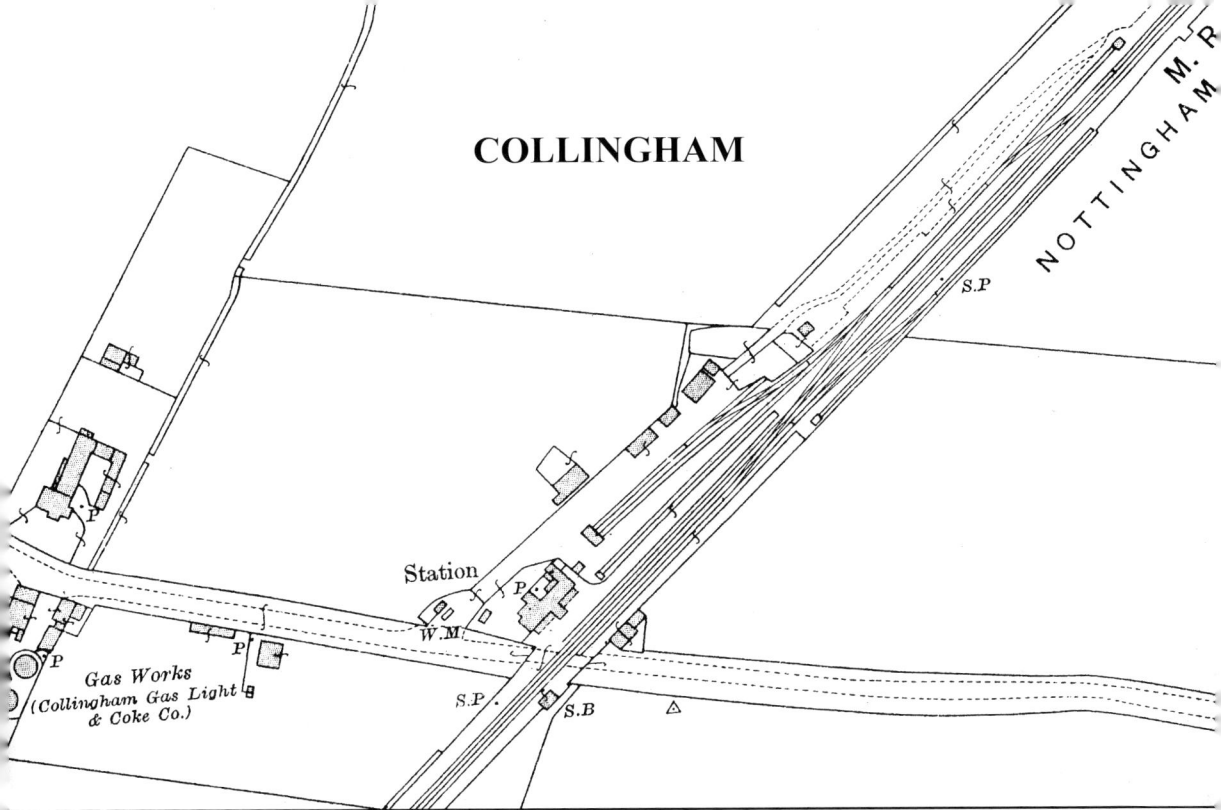

COLLINGHAM

XIII.   The 1920 edition shows the complex plan of the main building. The goods yard remained in use until 27th April 1964.

57.   A slightly damaged postcard reveals the complex Italianate styling, plus the single gate system. To the west was Winthorpe station in 1846-47. (P.Laming coll.)

58. The south end is seen again, but in 1965, when passenger access was direct to the platform. The station was unstaffed from 2nd November 1969. Carrots had been a notable item of goods outward, along with livestock.
(T.J.Edgington/ R.S.Carpenter coll.)

59. The goods shed was unusual in that it was attached to the waiting room. It is on the up platform and can be seen on the right of the previous picture. The platforms accommodate only two coaches.
(T.J.Edgington/ R.S.Carpenter coll.)

60. The 1965 survey is completed with this view of the signal box, which functioned until 11th September 1967. The south gate is also included.
(T.J.Edgington/ R.S.Carpenter coll.)

61.   No. 158848 runs through on 23rd June 1999, working the 15.05 Nottingham to Lincoln service. The waiting shelters are brick built and the platforms vary in height along their length, unusual by that time. The signal box stands, boarded up. (A.C.Hartless)

WEST OF SWINDERBY

62.   The sign states SOUTH SCARLE CROSSING and it is seen in 1955. It is only ¼ mile from Swinderby and was fitted with automatic half barriers later. On 6th June 1928, the Royal Mail train from Lincoln was derailed near here, killing one and injuring 16. (Stations UK)

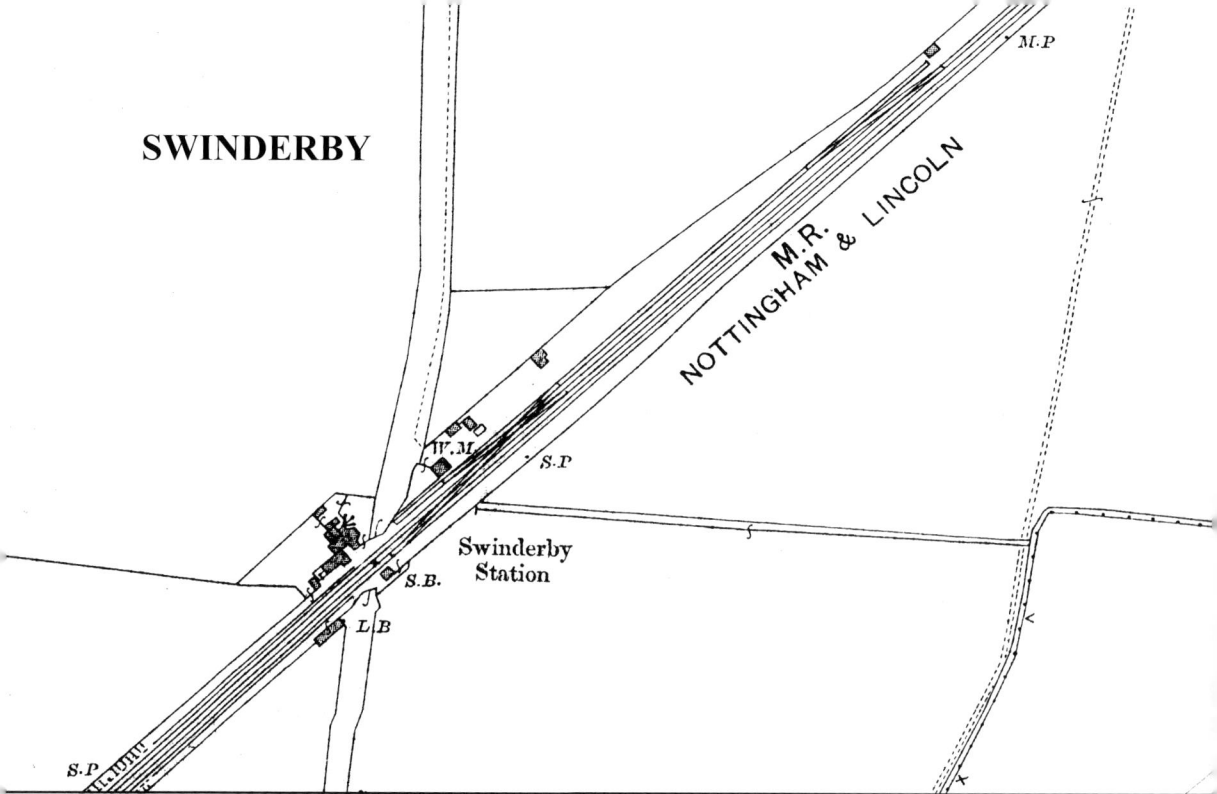

SWINDERBY

M.R.
NOTTINGHAM & LINCOLN

M.P

W.M.

S.P

Swinderby
Station

S.B.

L.B

S.P

XIV.   This was another station remote from habitation in a flat landscape and is shown on this 1919 edition. W.M. indicates weighing machine and L.B. a letterbox.

63.   A well composed postcard view includes cattle wagons with white patches. These were due to the limewash used for hygiene. Here again, there were single gates across the highway. (P.Laming coll.)

64.   One horsepower local transport can be enjoyed, along with superb architecture, which includes effective draught generating chimneys. The station was opened on 1st May 1847. (P.Laming coll.)

65.   A record from 7th August 1959 includes one of the fleet of DMUs introduced on 14th April 1958. It is working from Nottingham to Lincoln St. Marks. (Milepost 92½)

66.   A panorama from November 1965 features the goods shed, which had ceased to be used on 15th June 1964. The signal box was built in about 1901 and had 16 levers. (R.S.Carpenter)

67.   No. 156403 arrives on 7th September 2007, while working a Lincoln to Leicester service. The gates were still hand worked. The station had been unstaffed since 2nd November 1969. The down platform takes four coaches and the up three. (J.Whitehouse)

THORPE-ON-THE-HILL

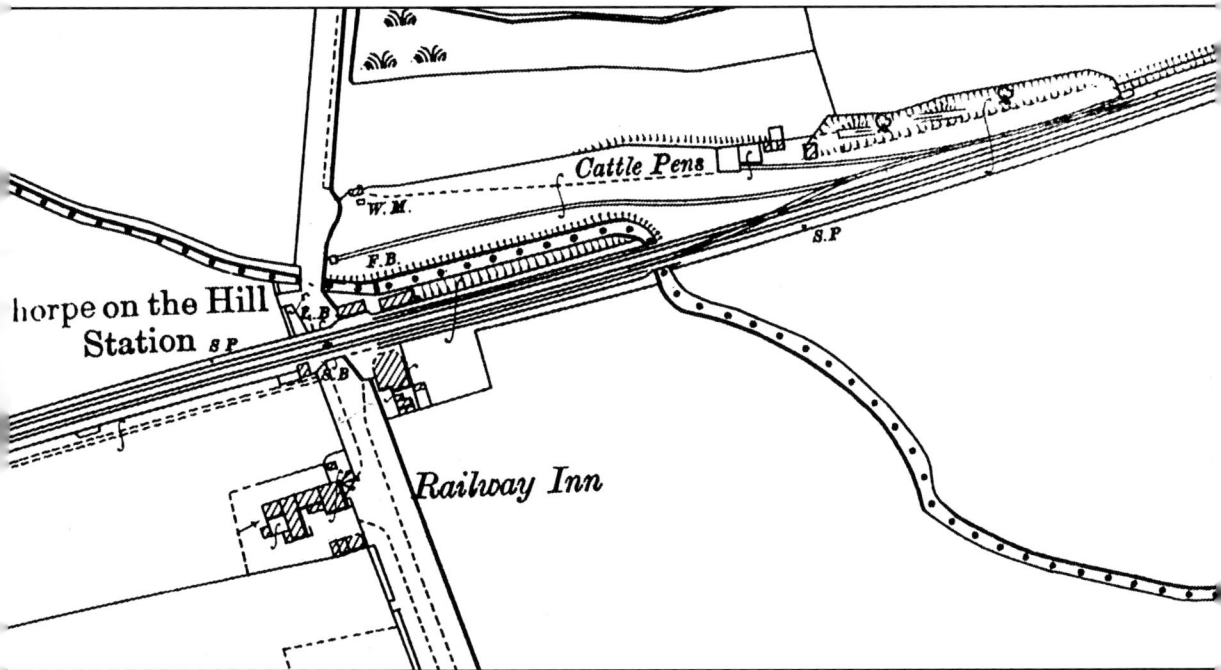

XV.   The 1905 map shows the name without hyphens; it did not have the suffix until 1st October 1890.

68.   The station building is now in residential use and the platforms have gone, as have the gates. The photograph is from 20th June 1953. (Milepost 92½)

69.   We look west in 1955 and see that the crossing had only two gates, instead of four. The signal box had a 16-lever frame and was in use until 18th March 1988. The building on the right was demolished in 1958. (Stations UK)

70.   The station was the most unprofitable one on the route and was closed on 7th February 1955, although the goods yard was open until 15th June 1964. Its cattle pen is visible in the background of this 1955 view. (Stations UK)

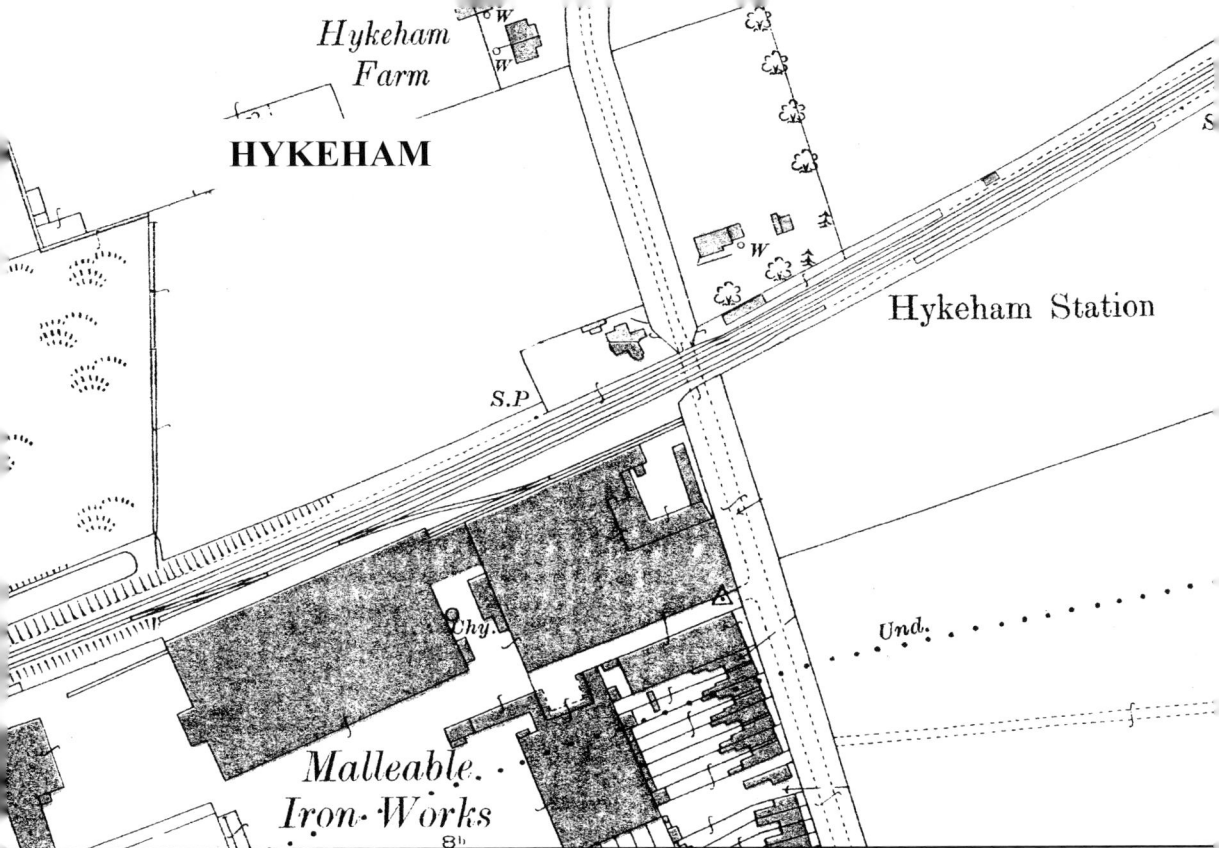

HYKEHAM

Hykeham Farm

Hykeham Station

S.P.

Chy.

Und.

Malleable Iron Works

XVI.   The 1932 edition reveals the extent of the private sidings and shows staggered platforms.

71.   An early postcard view includes a two-lever frame, which later had six. The signals protected the level crossing. The station had opened on 1st January 1849. (P.Laming coll.)

72.   A 1936 record confirms the staggering of the platforms. Public goods traffic began later, but it was discontinued on 16th June 1964. (Lens of Sutton coll.)

73.   The long siding has been shortened, but the up platform remains remote. No. 42333 is one of the BR-built 2-6-4Ts, introduced by the LMS in 1945. The picture is from 19th May 1957. (Milepost 92½)

74.   A photograph from the 1960s reveals that there were only two gates. These would be sufficient to close across the road. The siding buffer stops are beyond the left one. The station became unstaffed on 2nd November 1969. (Lens of Sutton coll.)

75.   Two shelters are seen to provide the passengers' requirements in March 2013. The crossing now has automatic half barriers and there is still a large factory behind the camera. (K.Knott)

WEST OF LINCOLN ST. MARKS

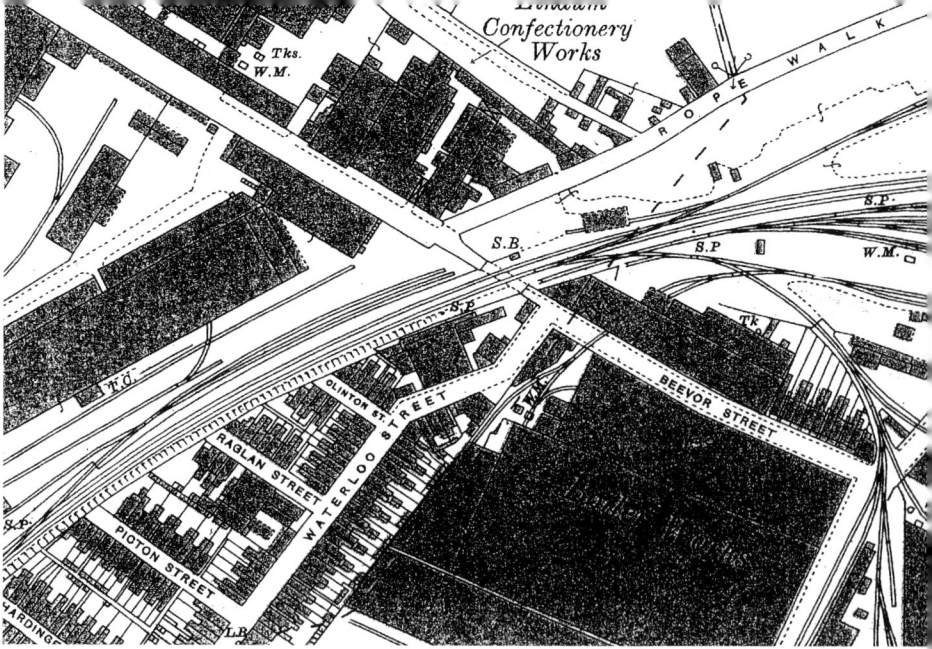

XVIIa. This location can be found on the left page of map XIX. The industries of the city were diverse, but agricultural and civil engineering equipment were high on the list. The factories were served by 24 private sidings in 1904. The 1932 extract is at 20ins to 1 mile.

76. Built and working in Lincoln was Ruston's 0-4-0ST no.1246/11. It was photographed in 1937 and moved away to Sheffield in 1954.
(J.K.Williams coll.)

XVIIb. The MR diagram is from about 1920. The passenger station is the largest rectangle.

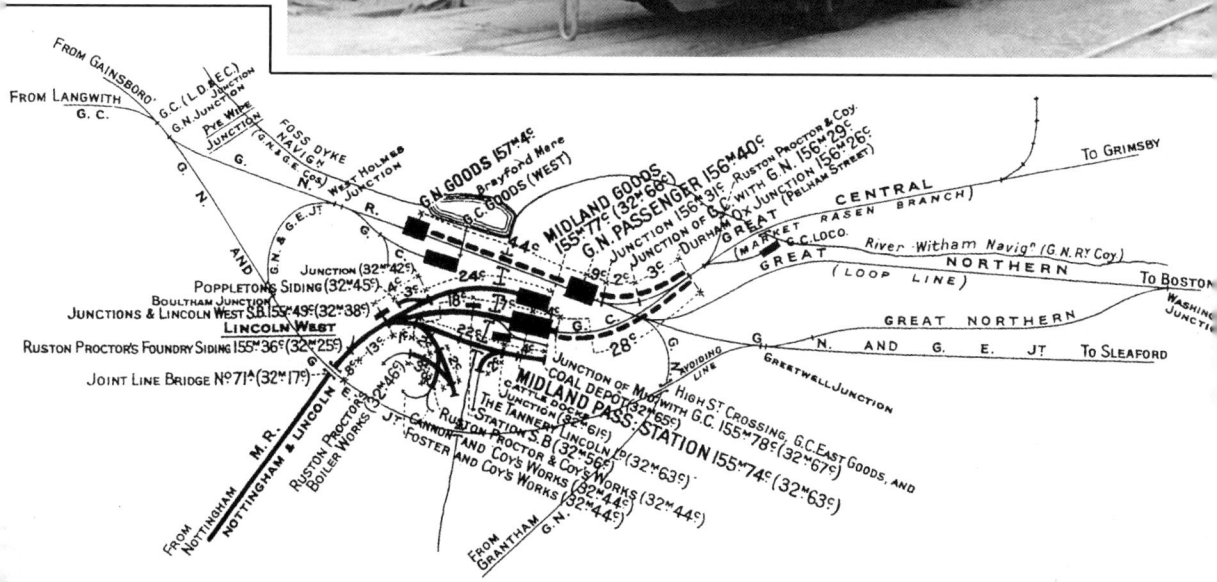

**LINCOLN
ST. MARKS**

77.   The station had a staff of 37 soon after it was opened and it was the first in the city. Good weather protection was on offer from the outset and under it on 8th June 1926 is ex-MR 2-4-0 no. 184 with the 3.0pm to Nottingham. (H.C.Casserley)

78.   It is now 24th April 1954 and class D11 4-4-0 no. 62666 *Zeebrugge* waits to leave for Nottingham at 5.0pm. On the right is the goods yard, which closed on 3rd May 1965. (H.C.Casserley)

BRAYFORD

Lucy Tower
(Site of)

Crane

BRAYFORD HEAD

Brayford Bridge

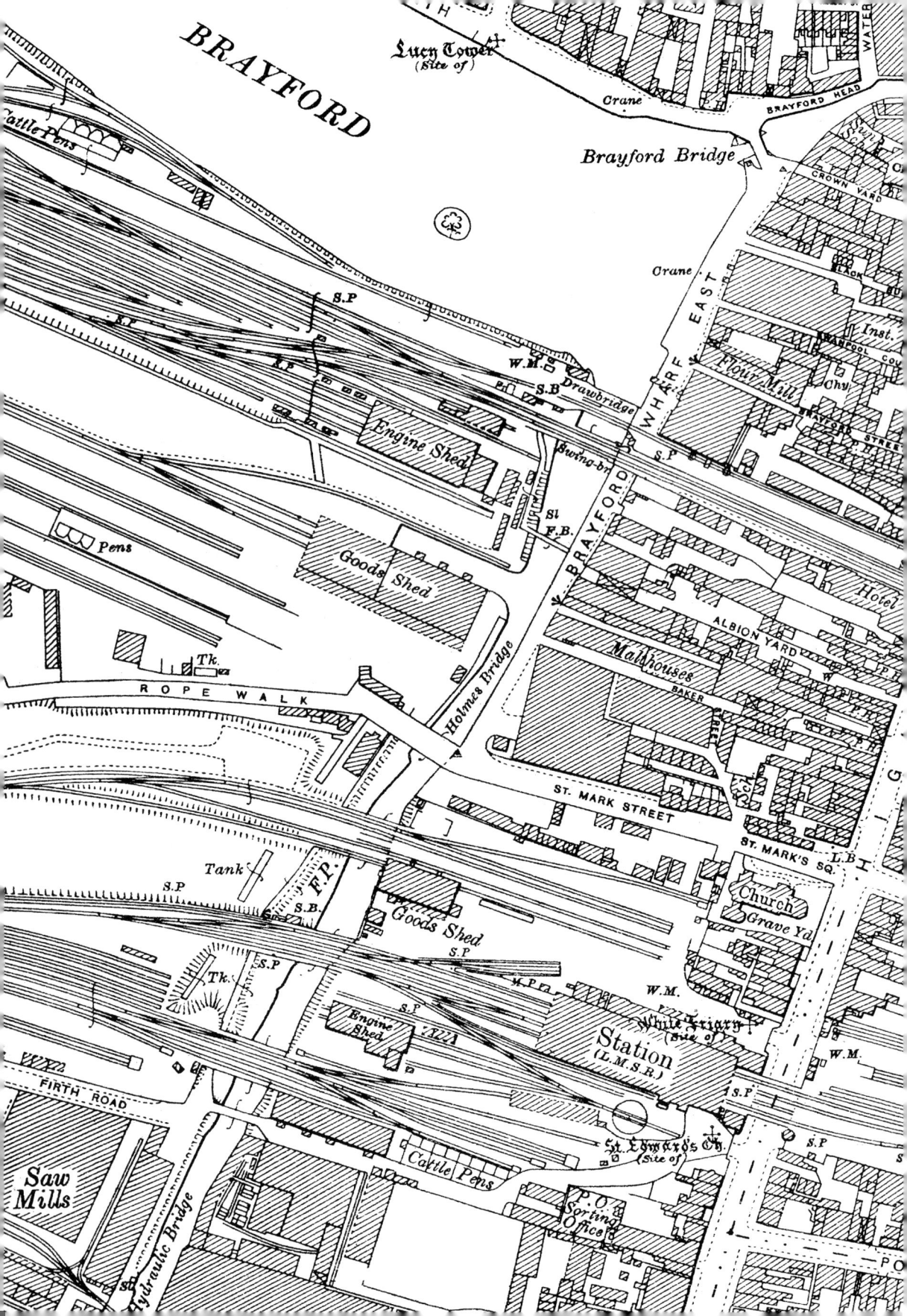

CROWN YARD

Cattle Pens

WHARF EAST

Crane

Inst.

Flour Mill

Chy

S.P

W.M.

S.B   Drawbridge

Engine Shed

Swing-b.

BRAYFORD

S.P

Hotel

Sl
F.B.

Pens

ALBION YARD

Goods
Shed

Malthouses

BAKER

Holmes Bridge

Tk.

ROPE WALK

ST. MARK STREET

ST. MARK'S SQ.

L.B.

Tank

Church
Grave Yd

FP.

S.P

S.B.

Goods Shed

S.P

Tk.

S.P

W.M.

Engine
Shed

White Friary
(Site of)

S.P

W.M.

W.M.

Station
(L.M.S.R.)

FIRTH ROAD

St. Edward's Ch.
(Site of)

S.P

Saw
Mills

Cattle Pens

P.O.
Sorting
Office

Hydraulic Bridge

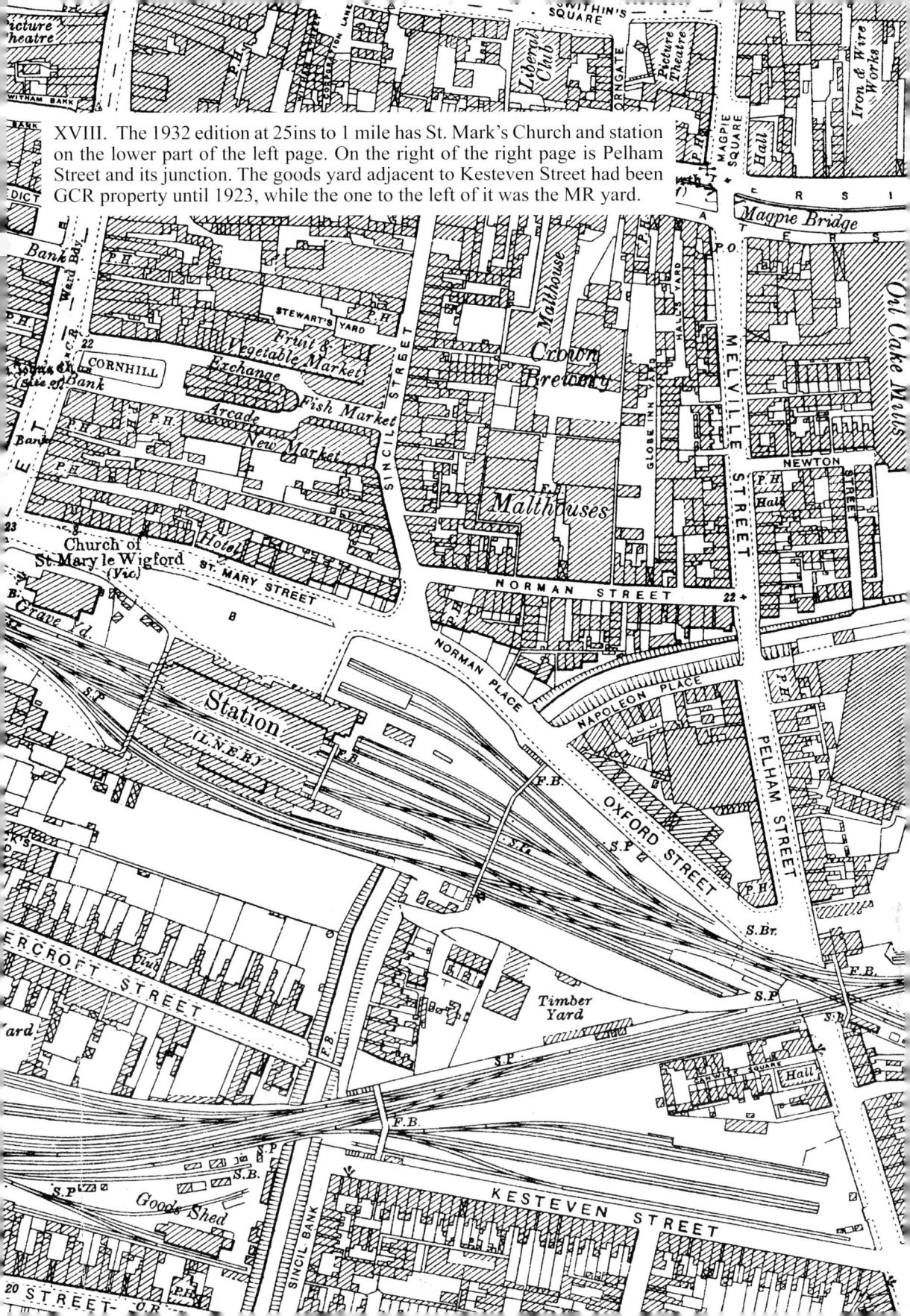

XVIII. The 1932 edition at 25ins to 1 mile has St. Mark's Church and station on the lower part of the left page. On the right of the right page is Pelham Street and its junction. The goods yard adjacent to Kesteven Street had been GCR property until 1923, while the one to the left of it was the MR yard.

79.   A view over the High Street on 2nd
September 1955 shows only one of the four
tracks originally laid across it. The smoke
stains show that two were still in use. The
other two were then used as sidings under
the roof. (H.C.Casserley)

80.   The ex-MR engine shed closed in
January 1959 and is seen in June 1961, along
with the southwest corner of the station.
West Signal Box is on the other side of the
river and is in the distance. It had 16 levers
and closed on 13th May 1985, along with
East Box and the station. (R.S.Carpenter)

→ 81. The ex-GCR coal depot can be found lower
right on map XVIII and is seen on 7th October 1976.
Modern coal handling equipment can be seen, as no.
03021 passes by with a barrier wagon. The down
direction is from Nottingham. (T.Heavyside)

↘ 82. The end of the route from Nottingham is
on the right, it having passed through St. Marks.
The lines from Lincoln Central are in the foreground
and on the right is Pelham Street Junction Box. In
front of it is no. 40143 with the 13.22 Skegness to
Manchester on 28th July 1979. The Grimsby route
is on the left and Greetwell Junction Box is in the
distance. (T.Heavyside)

83.   An eastward panorama in about 1967 has the gates in the distance, with the carriage sidings and servicing platforms in the centre. The DMU is waiting to leave for Nottingham. Although the roof vanished, the buildings survived. (M.J.Stretton)

84.   The north elevation was photographed in August 2008, it having been incorporated into a shopping centre. (Milepost 92½)

LINCOLN CENTRAL

85.   Seen on 2nd August 1958 is the impressive ex-GNR station of 1848. Departing east is class K3 2-6-0 no. 61890, a type which was introduced by the LNER in 1924. The tanks on the left were used for gas for kitchen cars. There are four bay platforms on the right. (Bentley coll.)

86.   Another westward view and this shows all four through platforms in 1961, when the population was 77,000. It was only about 14,000 in the 1840s. (Stations UK)

BALLAST HOLES

Golf Course

L.N.E.R. *March & Doncaster*

Allotment Gardens

L.N.E.R. *Boultham Curve*

Holmes West Junction

Boultham Junction

Pumping Engine House

Swan Pool

Allotment Gardens

Parly. Boro. By.

Allotment Gardens

Spike Island Works

NEW BOULTHAM

Boultham Leather Wks.

Confectionery Wks.

Boultham Works

Schools

Allotment Gardens

Mission Hall

War Meml.

L I N C O L N

XIX.   The 1933 survey at 6ins to 1 mile has the LMS route to Nottingham lower left and its station to the left of the High Street. The suffix "St. Marks" was used for it from 29th September 1950 until 12th May 1985, when a curve was opened between the O of LINCOLN and Boultham Junction. All trains thereafter used the ex-LNER one which is shown to the right of the High Street and was termed "Central" between those dates. The curve between Ballast Holes (left) and Cow Paddle (right) was a GNR/GCR joint venture in 1882 to form a bypass, but it was closed in 1983. Top left is the Gainsborough line and below it is the Chesterfield route. On the right border, from the top: Grimsby, Boston and Sleaford, with the Grantham route at the lower border.

RB

CATHEDRAL

Church
Parish Hall
Eastwood House
Monks Manor
The Dell
Caradoc Ho.
Lindum House
St. Anne's Chapel
Lindum Lodge
Lodge
Coldbath House
ASSIZE COURT County Court
The Lawn 202·7
The Quarry
The Mount
B.M. 217·7
Deanery
D'Isney Place
Vicarage
School
Band Stand
ARBORETUM
School
Abattoir
College
CATTLE MARKET
St. Joseph's School
Lincoln Avenue
Unity Sq.
Schs. 29·9
Schs.
Lucy Tower (Site of)
Brayford Bridge
BRAYFORD
Goods Shed
Station
Broadgate
Weirs
Lock
Mion Hall
F.B.
Titanic Bridge
Titanic Works
Sheaf Iron Works
Engineering Works
Stamp End Works
Engine Shed
Pelham Street Junction S.P.
Allotment Gardens
Globe Engineering Works
L.N.E.R.
MARCH & DONCASTER
Sports Ground
Mortuary
COW PADDLE
Trough
CANWICK ROAD NEW CEMETERY
Chaplin Street
King Street
Chelmsford Street
Monson Street
Ripon Street
Kirkby
Cranwell St.
Inn
Allotment Gardens
Lodge
Mortuary
CANWICK ROAD OLD CEMETERY
Mort. Chapels
Lodge
Hydraulic Ram
CANWICK
Canwick
Football Ground
Recreation Ground
Pav.
Allotment Gardens
Queen Street
Shakespeare Street
Gibbeson Street
Spencer Street
Golf Club House
L.N.E.R.
BARKSTON & LINCOLN
Lincoln 1
Sleaford 18
B.M. 34·1
B.M. 51·1
B.M. 114
Sewage Beds
Lodge
ROMAN PAVEMENT (Site of)
Canwick House

87.   We are at the west end of the station in June 1994, close to High Street Signal Box, which was still in use in 2013. Both through platforms take seven cars. (C.L.Caddy)

88.   High Street crossing is in the background as no. 158777 leaves, forming the 12.30 to Leicester via Nottingham on 2nd November 2012. The lines on the left serve the bay platforms. (P.Jones)

89.   A little further west and we stand on Brayford Wharf East (see centre of the map on the previous page) on 14th June 2008 to see ex-GWR 4-6-0 no. 5029 *Nunney Castle* pass East Holmes Signal Box. Behind the train are up and down goods loops and in the foreground is the River Witham. (J.Whitehouse)

Extract from Bradshaw's Guide for 1866.
(Reprinted by Middleton Press 2011).
See page 382 for more details therein.

Southwell to Mansfield
SOUTHWELL

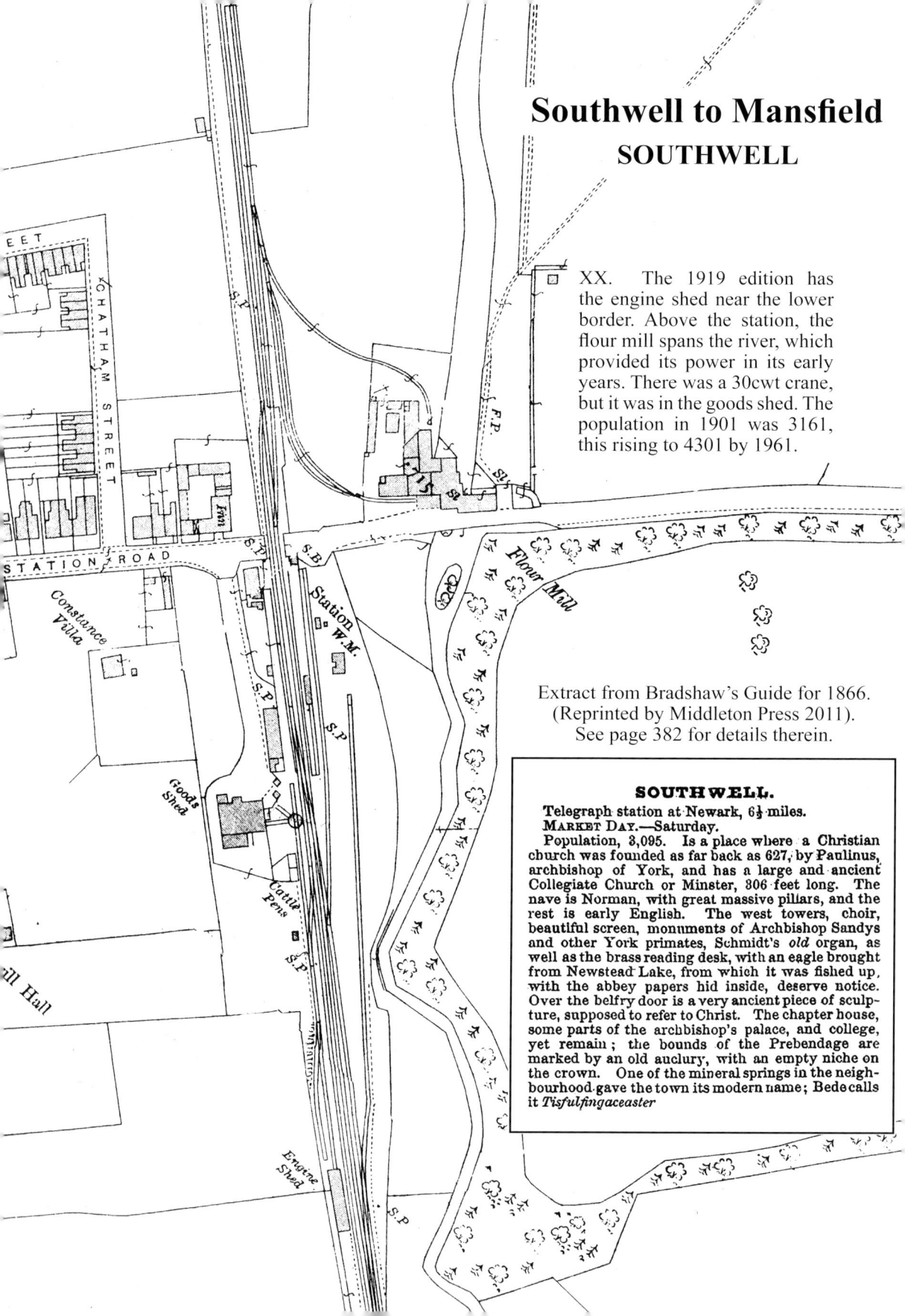

XX. The 1919 edition has the engine shed near the lower border. Above the station, the flour mill spans the river, which provided its power in its early years. There was a 30cwt crane, but it was in the goods shed. The population in 1901 was 3161, this rising to 4301 by 1961.

CHATHAM STREET

EET

STATION ROAD

Inn

S.P.

S.P.

S.B.

Station W.M.

Constance Villa

Goods Shed

Cattle Pens

ll Hall

Engine Shed

S.P.

S.P.

S.P.

F.P.

Sl.

Flour Mill

Extract from Bradshaw's Guide for 1866.
(Reprinted by Middleton Press 2011).
See page 382 for details therein.

SOUTHWELL.

Telegraph station at Newark, 6½ miles.

MARKET DAY.—Saturday.

Population, 3,095. Is a place where a Christian church was founded as far back as 627, by Paulinus, archbishop of York, and has a large and ancient Collegiate Church or Minster, 306 feet long. The nave is Norman, with great massive pillars, and the rest is early English. The west towers, choir, beautiful screen, monuments of Archbishop Sandys and other York primates, Schmidt's *old* organ, as well as the brass reading desk, with an eagle brought from Newstead Lake, from which it was fished up, with the abbey papers hid inside, deserve notice. Over the belfry door is a very ancient piece of sculpture, supposed to refer to Christ. The chapter house, some parts of the archbishop's palace, and college, yet remain; the bounds of the Prebendage are marked by an old auclury, with an empty niche on the crown. One of the mineral springs in the neighbourhood gave the town its modern name; Bede calls it *Tisfulfingaceaster*

90.   The spacious goods shed is on the right; a siding ran its entire width. The branch opened this far from the south on 1st July 1847, but the passenger service ceased from 1st August 1849 until 12th April 1852 and again from 14th March 1853 to 1st September 1860. (P.Laming coll.)

91.   The level crossing and the station masters house feature on a postcard franked in January 1914. By that period, the flour mill was steam powered, the tower being topped with a water tank. The 1885 signal box is evident; its 1926 successor was on the other side of the road and is just visible in picture 95. (P.Laming coll.)

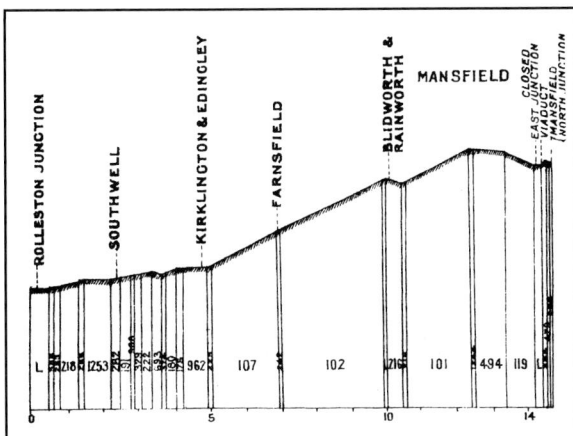

92.   This is a rare photograph from 1941, when photography was risky on grounds of security. Peace prevails as 0-4-4T no. 1344 waits to depart on 17th December. The south gable barge boards can be enjoyed. (H.C.Casserley)

93.   Starting signals both sides indicate bidirectional running on the right. The engine shed is in the distance in this view from 1948. No. 3529 is an 0-6-0 of LMS class 3F. The waiting rooms on both platforms were built in 1874. (Stations UK)

94.   Seen in about 1953 is 0-4-4T no. 58085 with LMS autocoach no. M2440TM. The shed became unsafe after an accident in March 1956 and was not used thereafter. Official closure for regular use was 10th January 1955. (P.J.Garland/R.S.Carpenter)

95.   A northward view on 2nd September 1955 includes 0-6-0 no. 64245 of class J6, ready to leave for Newark. The extension north to Mansfield opened in 1871, as deep coal mines were being planned. The route was single track, whereas the others in this album were double from the outset. (R.M.Casserley)

96.　　A southward panorama on 31st May 1958 has Upton Road Crossing Box in the distance. Centre is the engine shed, which was demolished in 1959. Goods traffic ceased here on 7th December 1964. (R.S.Carpenter)

97.　　It is dusk on 13th June 1959 and we witness the last passenger train to leave. The coach was hauled by 0-4-4T no. 58065. Official closure was two days later. The route south closed for freight in 1966. (D.A.Johnson)

KIRKLINGTON

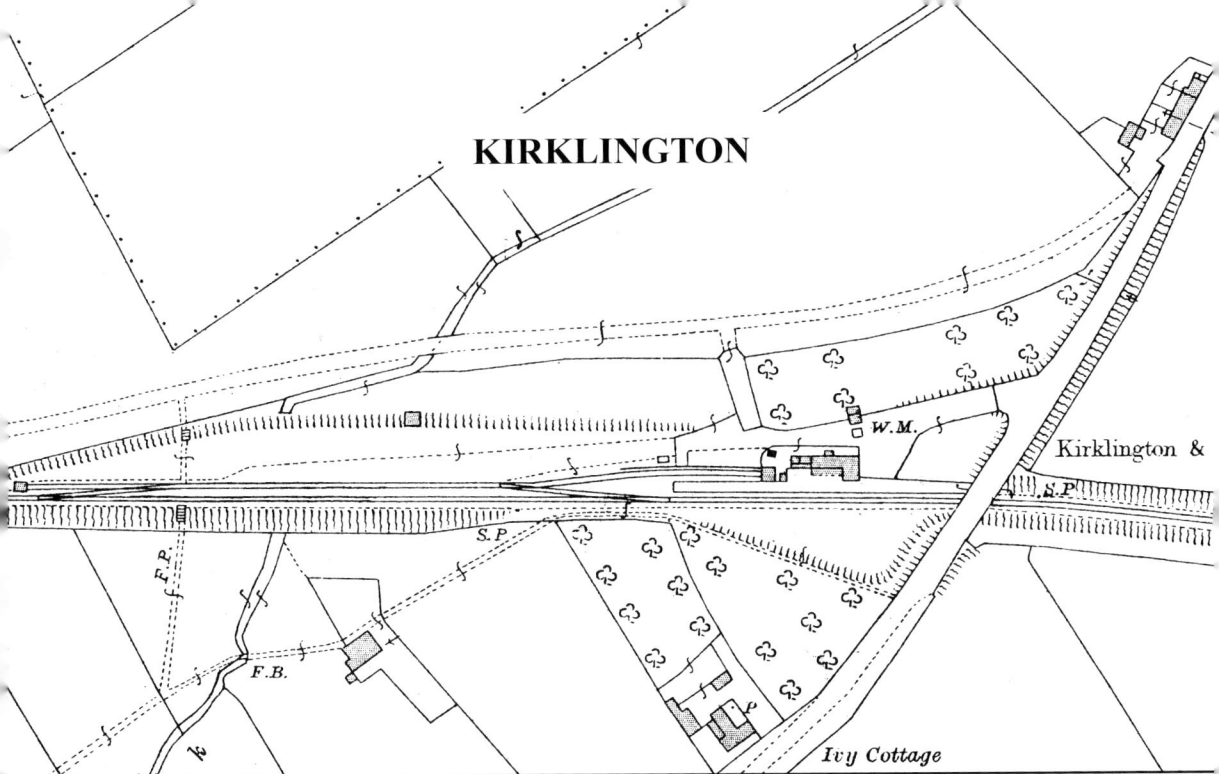

Kirklington &

XXI.   The 1920 extract includes part of the suffix "& Edlingly", although this was used only until 1st April 1904. There were 182 residents in 1901 and 228 in 1961.

98.   The fine building is seen in about 1905. This station and the two to the north of it were closed to passengers on 12th August 1929. (P.Laming coll.)

99.   The goods yard was overgrown when photographed in 1948, but it remained in use until 25th May 1964. It had a 3-ton capacity crane listed in 1938. (Stations UK)

BRITISH RLYS. (E)   BRITISH RLYS. (E)
For conditions   For conditions
   see back   see back
Available for three days Available for three days
including day of issue.   including day of issue.
Burton Joyce   Burton Joyce
BURTON JOYCE to
LINCOLN(ST.
MARKS)
LINCOLN St.M   LINCOLN St.M
3rd. 5s.8d.Z   3rd.

7634   7634

L. M. & S. R.
FOR CONDITIONS SEE NOTICES
CHILD
BURTON JOYCE TO
NOTTINGHAM (L.MS.)
THIRD
CLASS   FARE -/6 P

1311

FARNSFIELD

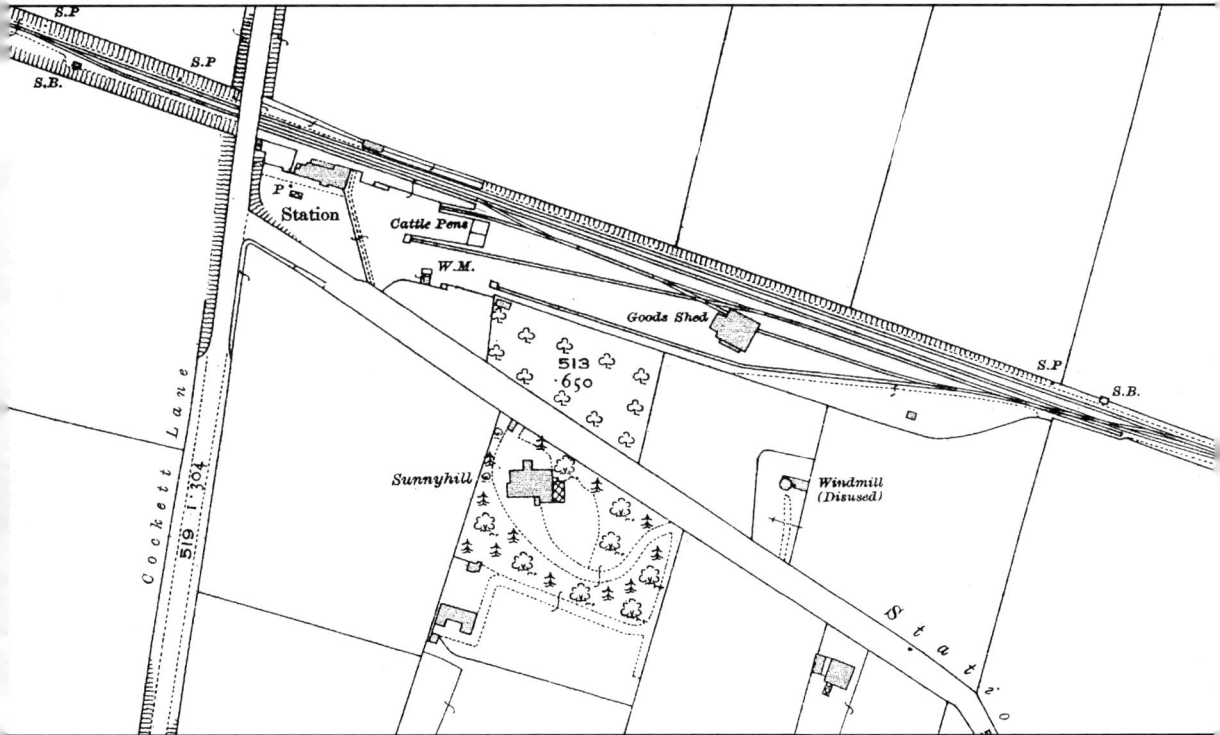

XXII.   The 1917 edition is at 20ins to 1 mile and here a siding ran through the goods shed. Two signal boxes are shown.

100.   A classic postcard view includes some fine finials and presentable prospective passengers posing. Residents in 1901 numbered 921. (Lens of Sutton coll.)

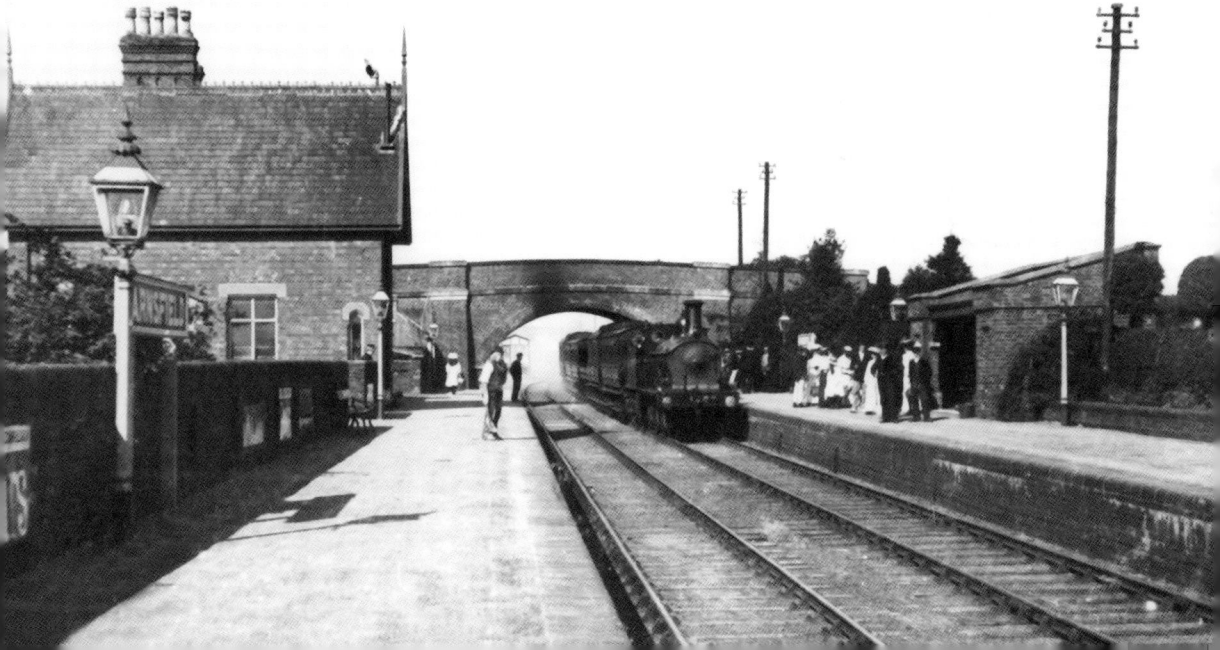

101.   A 1948 panorama includes East Box and two refuge sidings. They were mainly used for coal traffic. The goods yard was in use until 27th April 1964. (Stations UK)

NORTH OF FARNSFIELD

102.   Bilsthorpe Colliery was sunk in 1927 and sadly recorded a roof fall in 1993, which killed three. Closure followed in 1997. It was also served by an ex-GCR link from the west and the north-south joint LMS/LNE line of 1931. This joined our route, a little to the east of Farnsfield. (picturethepast.org.uk)

BLIDWORTH AND RAINWORTH

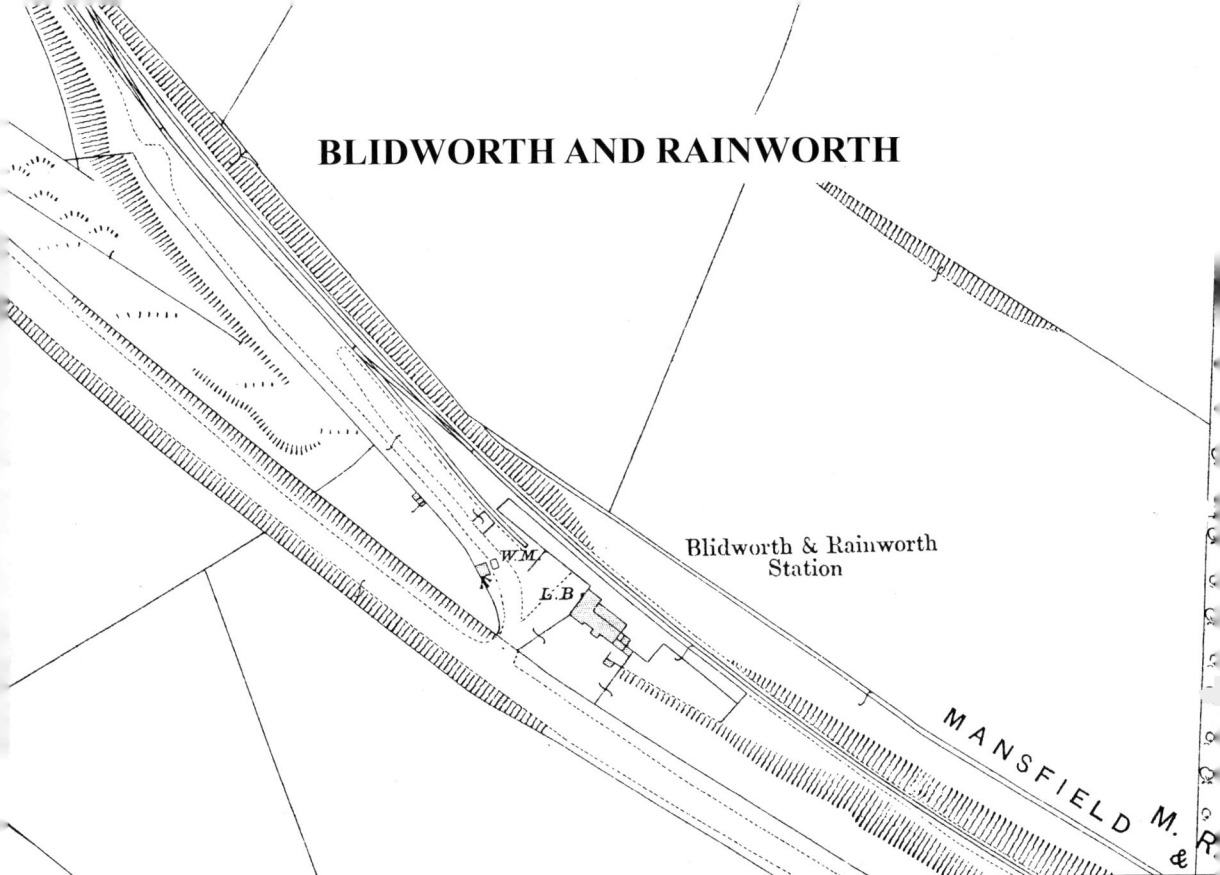

Blidworth & Rainworth
Station

MANSFIELD M. & R.

XXIII. The 1917 survey shows a long goods siding, but no passing loop.

103.   A damaged postcard posted in 1908 shows the name in use from 27th April 1894. Initially, it had been "Rainworth" and it was "Blidworth" from 1st May 1877. (P.Laming coll.)

104.   Here we look northwest in 1948. The number of souls in Blidworth was 1024 in 1901, this rising to 7308 in 1961. (Stations UK)

105.   Blidworth Colliery was on a branch south from the line from 1926 until 1984. New here in 1950 was Ruston, Stevens and Hornsby no. 7644, which was photographed in 1959 and scrapped on site in 1972. (J.K. Williams coll.)

106.   A tour train calls on 12th April 1952, headed by ex-MR class 4F 0-6-0 no. 44425. (Milepost 92½)

107.   Rufford Colliery had a branch north from the route. The pit was sunk in 1926 and was closed in 1984. Demolition was completed in 2006. (D.Bradbury/picturethepast.org.uk)

108.   Mansfield Colliery Junction is seen looking west on 16th July 1967. Mansfield Clipstone Colliery was in use from 1922 until 1988. (Milepost 92½)

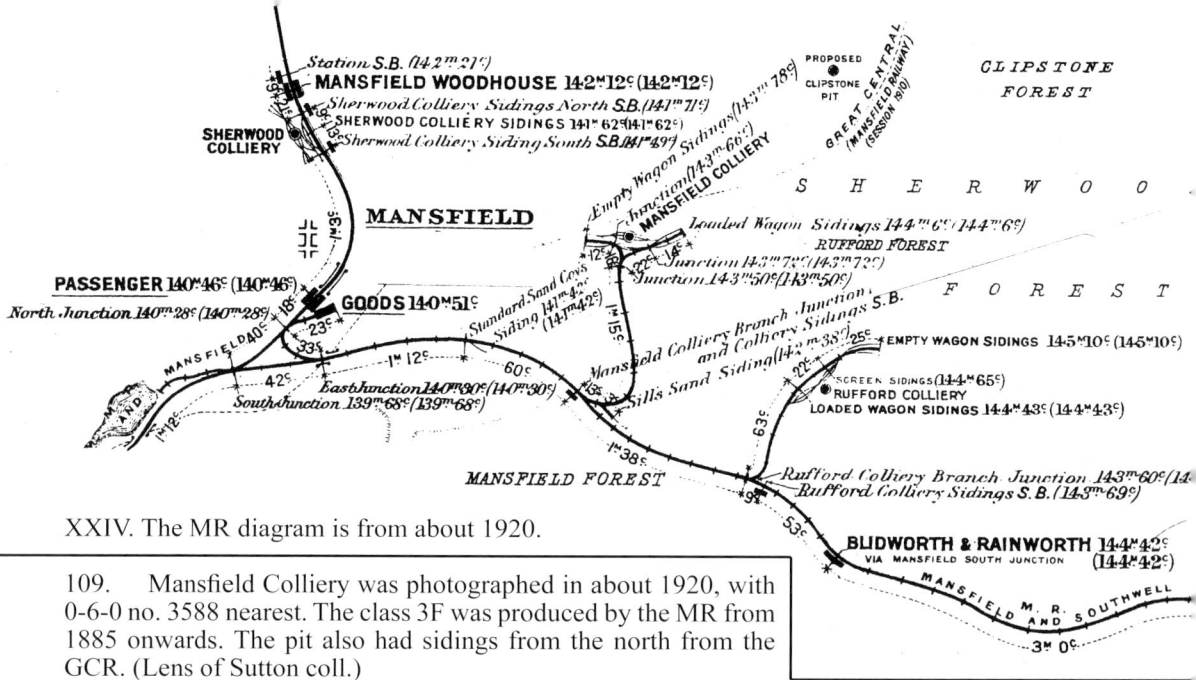

Station S.B. (142ᵐ21ᶜ)
MANSFIELD WOODHOUSE 142ᵐ12ᶜ (142ᵐ12ᶜ)
Sherwood Colliery Sidings North S.B. (141ᵐ71ᶜ)
SHERWOOD COLLIERY SIDINGS 141ᵐ62ᶜ(141ᵐ62ᶜ)
Sherwood Colliery Siding South S.B.(141ᵐ49ᶜ)

SHERWOOD COLLIERY

MANSFIELD

PASSENGER 140ᵐ46ᶜ (140ᵐ46ᶜ)
North Junction 140ᵐ28ᶜ (140ᵐ28ᶜ)
GOODS 140ᵐ51ᶜ
MANSFIELD 40

Standard Sand Co᷎s Siding 141ᵐ42ᶜ (141ᵐ42ᶜ)
East Junction 140ᵐ30ᶜ (140ᵐ30ᶜ)
South Junction 139ᵐ68ᶜ (139ᵐ68ᶜ)

Empty Wagon Sidings
Junction (143ᵐ78ᶜ)
MANSFIELD COLLIERY
Loaded Wagon Sidings 144ᵐ6ᶜ (144ᵐ6ᶜ)
RUFFORD FOREST
Junction 143ᵐ72ᶜ(143ᵐ72ᶜ)
Junction 143ᵐ50ᶜ(143ᵐ50ᶜ)
Mansfield Colliery Branch Junction and Colliery Sidings S.B.
Mansfield Colliery Branch Junction and Colliery Sidings(143ᵐ38ᶜ)
Sills Sand Siding
EMPTY WAGON SIDINGS 145ᵐ10ᶜ (145ᵐ10ᶜ)
SCREEN SIDINGS (144ᵐ65ᶜ)
RUFFORD COLLIERY
LOADED WAGON SIDINGS 144ᵐ43ᶜ (144ᵐ43ᶜ)
Rufford Colliery Branch Junction 143ᵐ60ᶜ(14...
Rufford Colliery Sidings S.B. (143ᵐ69ᶜ)

MANSFIELD FOREST

PROPOSED CLIPSTONE PIT
GREAT CENTRAL (MANSFIELD RAILWAY) (SESSION 1910)

CLIPSTONE FOREST

S H E R W O O

F O R E S T

BLIDWORTH & RAINWORTH 144ᵐ42ᶜ (144ᵐ42ᶜ)
VIA MANSFIELD SOUTH JUNCTION
MANSFIELD AND SOUTHWELL M.R.
3ᵐ 0ᶜ

XXIV. The MR diagram is from about 1920.

109.   Mansfield Colliery was photographed in about 1920, with 0-6-0 no. 3588 nearest. The class 3F was produced by the MR from 1885 onwards. The pit also had sidings from the north from the GCR. (Lens of Sutton coll.)

110.   Named *Thoresby No. 1*, this Hawthorn Leslie 0-4-0ST was built in 1925 and came to Mansfield Colliery in about 1935. It was pictured in 1955 and cut up on site in 1964. (J.K.Williams coll.)

SOUTH OF MANSFIELD

111. Mansfield North Junction is on the left page of the next map. This and the next two pictures were taken in August 1964. The station is in the distance. (Milepost 92½)

112. Mansfield East Junction is seen. The line to South Junction was in use in 1906-83. The route to Rufford Junction also closed in 1983. The locomotive is no. 44248 and it is hauling a Blidworth to Woodhouse Mill mineral train, while tokens are exchanged. The box had 44 levers. (Milepost 92½)

113. Mansfield South Junction is now visited. The route between it and North Junction was open from 1871 to 1966. The zero milepost is on the left of this picture, which shows "Black 5" no. 45253 approaching with a Skegness to Radford train. (Milepost 92½)

MANSFIELD

XXV. The 1917 survey has the route from Southwell lower left, from Nottingham top left and Yorkshire top right. All were MR lines. The station was initially a terminus and was south of the goods shed in 1849-72.

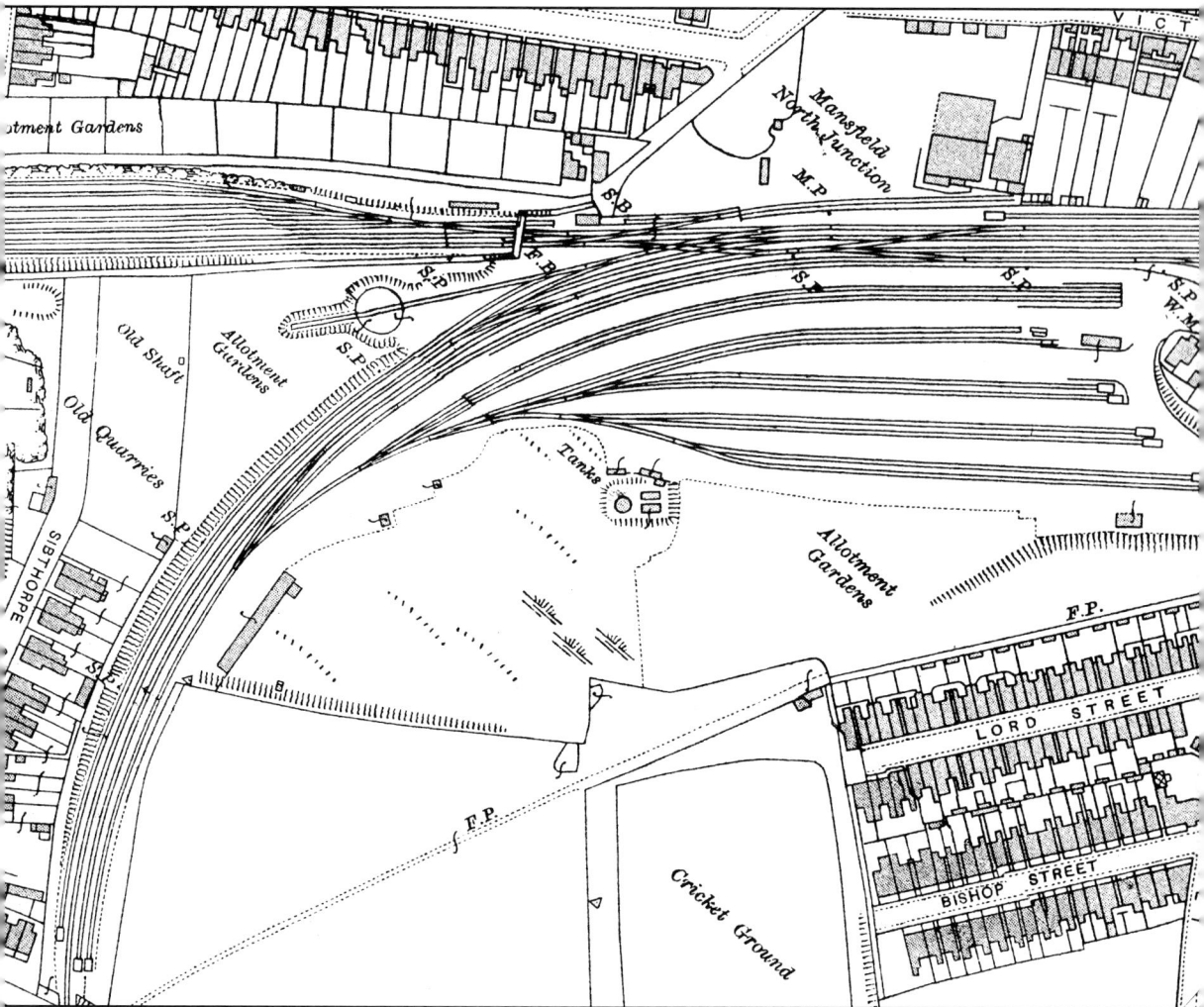

The street tramway, lower right, was that of Mansfield & District Light Railway Co Ltd and was in use from 1899 until 1932.

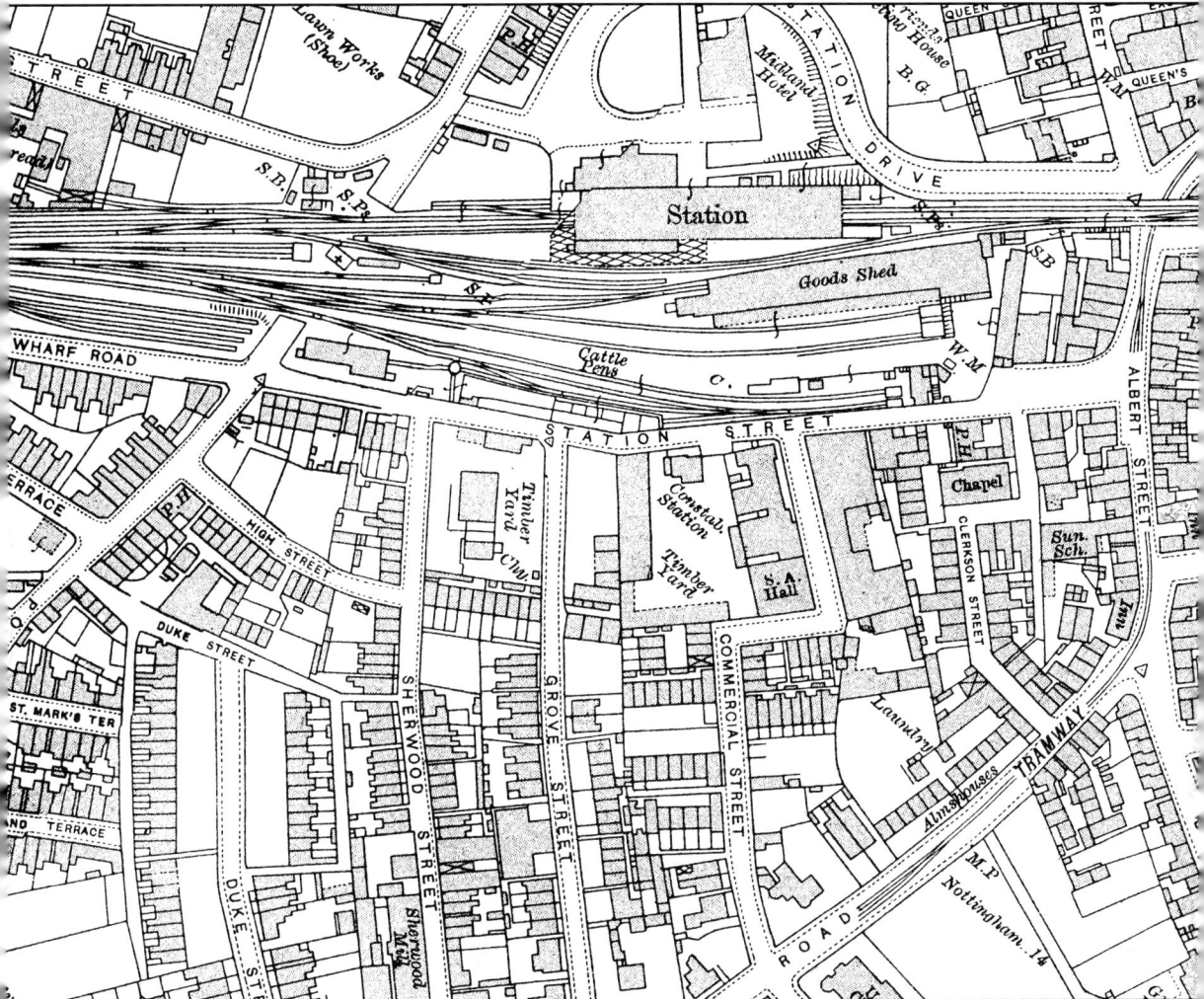

114.   The passenger entrance is on the north side of the spacious station, facing the town centre. The suffix "Town" was added on 11th August 1952, although the goods depot was so named on 1st July 1950. (P.Laming coll.)

115.   The replacement bus service for the Southwell-Mansfield trains began at Newark and started on 28th August 1929. The buses ran every 15 minutes during weekdays, a great improvement on a train twice a day. Coal trains could then become more frequent. (LMS Magazine)

116. The splendid roof was photographed in 1954, along with the roof of the subway (lower right) and the steps down to it, on the left. The population was 21,445 in 1901, it rising to 54,130 by 1961. (Stations UK)

117. Platforms 1, 2 and 3 are included in this record from 1955. No. 43727 was an 0-6-0 of a type introduced by the MR in 1885 and classified 3F. (Stations UK)

118.   The entrance to the goods yard is seen on 2nd August 1959. Freight traffic ceased here on 2nd June 1975. (Milepost 92½)

119.   A photograph from 5th May 1962 of the east end of the station includes class 4 2-6-4T no. 42232 waiting to depart and no. 48704 arriving. The station closed to passengers on 12th October 1964. (Milepost 92½)

120.   It is 8th May 1965 and we witness an LCGB tour from St. Pancras. It ran via Leicester, Skegness, Boston and Corby. (Milepost 92½)

L. M. & S. R.

issued subject to the conditions & regulations in the Co's Time Tables Books Bills & Notices.

FARNSFIELD to

MANSFIELD

THIRD CLASS.   3662(S)   FARE 1/0
Mansfield

MIDLAND RAILWAY. This Ticket is issued subject to the Regulations & Conditions stated in the Company's Time Tables & Bills.

THIRD CLASS.   THIRD CLASS.
AVAILABLE ON DAY OF ISSUE ONLY.

SOUTHWELL to

ROLLESTON JUNCTION

FARE 2½d   FARE 2½d.

Southwell-Rolleston J   Southwell-Rolleston J

MP Middleton Press
EVOLVING THE ULTIMATE RAIL ENCYCLOPEDIA

Easebourne Lane, Midhurst, West Sussex.
GU29 9AZ   Tel:01730 813169

www.middletonpress.co.uk   email:info@middletonpress.co.uk
A-978 0 906520   B- 978 1 873793   C- 978 1 901706   D-978 1 904474
E - 978 1 906008   F - 978 1 908174

All titles listed below were in print at time of publication - please check current availability by looking at our website - *www.middletonpress.co.uk* or by requesting a Brochure which includes our *LATEST* RAILWAY TITLES also our TRAMWAY, TROLLEYBUS, MILITARY and COASTAL series